Gender Discrimination and Development Paradox

Gender Discrimination and Development Paradox

Edited by

Neerja Ahlawat

RAWAT PUBLICATIONS

Jaipur • New Delhi • Bangalore • Guwahati • Kolkata

ISBN 978-81-316-0774-9

Published by
Prem Rawat for **Rawat Publications**
Satyam Apts., Sector 3, Jawahar Nagar, Jaipur 302 004 (India)
Phone: 0141 265 1748/7006 Fax: 0141 265 1748
E-mail: info@rawatbooks.com
Website: www.rawatbooks.com

New Delhi Office
4858/24, Ansari Road, Daryaganj, New Delhi 110 002
Phone: 011 2326 3290

Also at *Bangalore, Guwahati* and *Kolkata*

Typeset by Rawat Computers, Jaipur
Printed at Chaman Enterprises, New Delhi

To my soulmate
Sadhu Ram

Contents

Preface

Gender discrimination continues to perplex despite burgeoning socio-economic development. My active engagement with skewed child sex ratio and the missing girl child dates back to 2005 when Action Aid Study on 'Adverse Child Sex Ratio' was initiated and coaxed me to understand the dynamics of the persisting age-old adverse child sex ratios in India. This book is a testimony to the extent to which discrimination against the girl child and women continues.

Economic development along with dissemination of ideas and technologies and increasing reach of the media has made a big impact on society, social values and aspirations. The coming together of small family norm and rising economic aspirations has resulted in the persistence of some age-old practices and the adoption of new practices, e.g. demand for more dowry at the time of marriage and continuing demand after marriage – including in-laws pressuring the girl to seek her share of parental property. Well-meaning and gender just laws have mutated with greater pressure on married women. Therefore, dowry and its manifestations continue for many years after marriage.

The overall socio-economic development in India – particularly in terms of better standard of living, improved health care, specially maternal and infant and child health, increased life span, narrowed literacy level gaps between male and female, growing opportunities for work particularly for women – has not resulted in equalizing sex ratios in general and gender relations in particular. Rather, the child sex ratio declines are not only getting worse but taking newer forms and manifestations. In this ongoing process of transformation, there is a trend towards smaller families where sons are favoured desperately, deselecting daughters at any cost. The economically developed states with higher per capita income have shown a decline in sex ratio. The economically developed states have better infrastructure, and are therefore in a better position to provide scientific technologies of sex selection leading to a sharp decline in child sex ratio as evident from census information pertaining to child sex ratio in the developed states. People having higher incomes, urban based and highly educated have been found to indulge relatively in a higher extent of female foeticide.

Census 2011 has unfolded many interesting facts about India's sex ratio. What is shocking and disheartening is that though the overall sex ratio has improved nationwide from 933 in 2001 to 940 in 2011 Census, it shows dismal and shocking revelations about the child sex ratio in India as well as other states. It seems that people's intolerance for the girl child continues with the child sex ratio dipping alarmingly by 13 points to settle at 914 (against 927 girls per 1,000 boys between 0 and 6 years in 2001) – the lowest since 1961. The states of Haryana, Punjab, Delhi and the Union Territory of Chandigarh lead this dubious distinction, with sex ratios 830, 846, 866 and 867, respectively.

The book in its present form is the outcome of the seminars organized by Women's Studies Centre, M.D. University, Rohtak in collaboration with ICSSR North–West

Regional Centre, Chandigarh. I am thankful to the then Vice-Chancellor, Professor R.P. Hooda, for his constant encouragement.

Professor S.R. Ahlawat, my beloved husband deserves special appreciation for his invaluable suggestions and comments. The book, in its present form, would not have been completed without his support and interventions. I express my deep sense of gratitude to my children Ajay, Priya, Priyanka and Nikhil for their love and affection. I am extremely grateful to all the contributors for having readily agreed to be a part of this volume. The present endeavour could not have been completed without their cooperation. I am sure the book will be of great value to students, researchers, academicians and policy-makers. My special thanks are due to Rawat Publications for the publication of this book.

Neerja Ahlawat

Contributors

Anjali Radkar, Professor, Gokhale Institute of Politics and Economics, Pune.

Anjali Dewan, Head, Department of Home Science, St. Bede's College, Shimla.

Binod Mishra, Assistant Professor, Department of Humanities and Social Sciences, Indian Institute of Technology–Roorkee, Uttarakhand.

Dweepika Kumari, Research Scholar, Department of Geography, Patna University, Bihar.

Jaya Kritika Ojha, Research Scholar, Department of Humanities and Social Sciences, Indian Institute of Technology–Roorkee, Uttarakhand.

Mary E. John, Senior Fellow, Centre for Women's Development Studies, New Delhi.

Manjeet Rathee, Professor, Department of English, Maharshi Dayanand University, Rohtak.

Mitu Khurana, AMS at Sri Balaji Action Medical Institute, New Delhi.

Neerja Ahlawat, Deputy Director, Women's Studies Centre, Maharshi Dayanand University, Rohtak.

Sonu Dehmiwal, Assistant Professor, Department of Law, Maharshi Dayanand University, Rohtak.

Sudha Yadav, Assistant Professor, Department of Sociology, Government College for Women, Chandigarh.

Virinder Singh, Senior Fellow, Centre for Research in Rural and Industrial Development, Chandigarh.

Introduction

Neerja Ahlawat

The unusually masculine sex ratio of India's population remains a matter of grave concern today. Earlier, it was attributed to higher mortality levels among females than males. However, the juvenile sex ratio shows massive declines in each census. The nationwide overall sex ratio (the number of females per thousand males) in 2011 Census has shown an improvement of seven points, i.e. from 933 in 2001 Census to 940 in 2011 Census. This is the highest sex ratio so far at the national level since 1971 Census. What is perplexing the minds of social scientists, demographers and policy planners is the further decline in child sex ratio from 927 in 2001 Census to 914 in 2011 Census. The Censuses 2001 and 2011 have shown sharp declines in CSR across India (18 and 13-point decline, respectively). It shows that intolerance towards the girl child continues despite the implementation of PCPNDT.

In recent decades, the worst gender ratios, indicating gross gender imbalance, are found in South and East Asian countries such as India and China. The pre-birth sex selection of the foetus by ultrasound scanning, amniocentesis, and in-vitro fertilization has aggravated this situation.

An estimated 117 million women across Asia are 'missing'. Although this trend is prevalent in countries of South Asia and South East Asia (India, Nepal, Pakistan, Bangladesh, China and Vietnam), yet the trend is catching up in Eastern Europe and Caucasus. Amartya Sen (1990) drew the attention of the nation towards the 'missing women phenomena' that with India's present population of one hundred and twenty crore people, we have to make an account of some 25 million 'missing women'. If western standards were applied, India too should have had about 105 women for every 100 men today. Thus, there should have been 512 million women in India. It has been estimated that approximately 0.5 million girls have been denied being born during the past two decades. According to a UNICEF report, nearly 50 million girls are missing from India's population.

India shares a distinctive feature of South Asian and Chinese populations with regard to male-female ratio: a centuries old deficit of females to males, the opposite of non-Asian countries. Of more serious concern to the country is that the sex ratio defined is the number of females per thousand males (which is opposite to the internationally used definition of males per thousand females) and has been consistently declining over past decades.

Both demographic and sociological literature has explored the reasons for increasing deficit of women/girls and emphasized that the main cause has been patriarchal social order resulting in women's lower status. Feudal mindset still dogs women's struggle and has led to a persistent survival disadvantage experienced by women from early childhood to their reproductive period. Many studies carried out since 1970s have shown how cultural practices have always under-valued daughters or women in Indian society. The neglect and discriminatory behaviour against girls leading to excess female mortality has been widely documented (Visaria, 1971; Dasgupta, 1987; Miller, 1989; Kishor, 1995). One-third of 12 million girls born every year in India die in their first year; 25 per cent do not survive beyond 15 years of age. There is strong evidence that given access to similar food, care and medical attention, fewer women and girls die at all ages than men and boys because they are biologically stronger. Yet, in India, more women and girls die than men and boys through childhood and their reproductive years up to the age of 30. Most of the deaths of girls are the result of neglect in terms of food, medical care, etc. Girls are breast-fed for shorter duration; they are taken to fewer medical consultations and often very late or never to the hospitals (Dreze and Sen, 1975). The risk faced by the girl child appears to be more acute in areas which have strongly benefited from the ongoing process of rapid economic change, and consequent considerable changes in the social fabric of society. Clearly, there is a stronger bias against the girl child, particularly among the rich and the educated Indians.

It is obvious that daughter aversion and son preference continues and it is widely prevalent in most parts of Indian society and this is expressed through rampant use of sex-selective technologies leading to abortions, neglect of female child and female infanticide (Sudha and Rajan, 1999). It follows that alongside the process of transformation, there is a trend towards smaller families favouring sons and deliberately choosing not to have daughters, especially the second one. Paradoxically, it seems that the phenomenon appears to increase with development. There is strong bias against the girl child particularly among educated, affluent and urban based families (Dyson and Moore, 1983; Dasgupta, 1987; Agnihotri, 2000; Bose, 2001). The economically developed states, e.g. Haryana and Punjab with higher per capita income have shown a consistent decline in child sex ratio. Since these states have better infrastructure, they are therefore in a better position to provide scientific technologies of sex selection leading to a sharp decline in child sex ratio as evident from Census 2011. The people with higher incomes, urban based and highly educated have been found to indulge in a relatively higher extent of female foeticide. Daughter discrimination and son preference has a long history and there are conscious strategies to plan families with sons and preferably without daughters (John et al., 2008).

Female Infanticide in India

Although female infanticide is an anachronism in modern times, yet it exists silently in many communities and regions of India. Historically, there has been a tradition of killing female child by feeding poisonous milk or suffocating the child or simply by ill-treating or neglect (Kynch and Sen, 1983). Despite stringent legislation against the practice of infanticide, it continues unabated in many parts of India. Infanticide is an act of killing a new-born with the consent of both or either of the parent or family members. Though it is a crime, it has cultural and traditional sanctions attached to it which are basically responsible for the continuation of this practice. There are strong historical evidences of the practice of female infanticide in British India particularly among higher castes in Northern India in the late 18th and 19th century. The killing of girl babies has a long history in North–West India and remains quite common in particular areas and communities (Premi and Raju, 1996). A special census report of 1881 showed that seven caste groups of North–Western Provinces of India were practising female infanticide and these were Jats, Gujjars, Tagas, Ahars, Rajputs, Minars and Ahirs.

Historically, the practice of female infanticide was limited to upper caste groups only mainly due to the prevalence of hypergamy (a practice where a woman is married to a man having better status than hers); parents often worried about the suitable match for their daughter (Sudha and Rajan, 1999). This practice was first reported by British official Jonathan Duncan in 1789 among Rajkumar Rajputs in Jaunpur district of Benaras division while he was touring the district for revenue purposes (Kaye, 1966). Some of the historical legends behind this traditional atrocious custom as reported by Pakrasi (1970) about the Jadejas of Gujarat, who occupied the top position in the Gujarati Rajput hierarchy, are of great interest. Colonel Walker, the British administrator who ruled Gujarat in early 19th century (1805–1825), reported that Jadejas never showed any hesitation in admitting the practice of infanticide. The Rajputs of Gujarat and Bhati caste of Jaisalmer in Rajasthan follow this murderous tradition even today. The Rajputs of Uttar Pradesh believed that 'a father who preserves a girl child will never live to see her suitably married or that the family she is married into will be ruined' (Miller, 1987). Barbara Miller (1981) in her analysis in the book on the 'endangered sex' reported that a higher rate of neglect of female children was prevalent among North Indians than South Indians. However, there have been cases of infanticide being reported in Tanu Manji in Tamil Nadu and the communities of Thevars (Kallars), Goundersand, Vanniyars from Madurai and Salem districts of the state (Mahadevan, 1979; Venkataramani, 1986; Rajaretnam, 1992). In Tamil Nadu, the districts of Madurai and Dharampuri have exceptionally few girls and have been in the news for the alleged murder of baby girls.

As regards the practice of infanticide, it was observed that different methods were employed to kill the baby girl immediately after birth. Among Rajputs, there was a practice of applying opium on the nipple of the mother's breasts for killing the female child. Another method used was to tie the umbilical cord around the neck of the female baby tightly till she dies. Immersing the baby into a vessel of milk known as 'Doodh Pilana' was also practised among Rajputs. In Kutch region, the female Rajgor (Brahmin) was supposed to kill the female baby and bury it too (Pakrasi, 1970). Among Bhatti caste of Rajasthan, the common practice was to kill the child with suffocation by burying into a bagful of sand or to kill her by feeding mother's milk with opium applied on her nipples. In case she still survived, she was strangulated.

In Tamil Nadu, a variety of methods were used to kill the female baby. There are instances being reported where the father of the baby stepped on the throat to kill her. Another way was to feed the baby with poisonous milk of a wild plant with little sugar (Calotopis Gigantea) or the Oleander Berries known for lethal poison. To kill the baby, the mouth was stuffed with grains of paddy along with honey. Feeding hot chicken gravy was another method used to kill the new-born female baby. There were also instances where sleeping pills were mixed with milk and fed to kill the baby girl. However, one of the latest and commonly used methods of killing the female baby is to wrap the baby tightly in a wet turkey towel and keep it in a corner for some time; the baby dies within a few minutes. It shows how direct infanticide has been practised for centuries and the way the crude methods are used to eliminate the newly-born baby girl. The reasons responsible for this practice are deep-rooted in socio-cultural and economic aspects of Indian society where birth of a son is essential, therefore celebrated, whereas birth of a daughter is viewed as a disgrace, lowering one's position in the patriarchal society.

Post-Independence Scenario

Though information on caste was discontinued immediately after Independence, it is possible to make some judgments based on the historical records of female infanticide with region-specific census data on sex ratio patterns observed since Independence. While undivided Punjab had certain caste groups known for killing the female child, after Independence it is now Punjab and Haryana that consistently show a decline in child sex ratio. Gujarat, Rajasthan and Uttar Pradesh are other states where some of the castes practised female infanticide; now they are the states that have a low child sex ratio (Premi, 2001). It shows that the practice of female infanticide which was confined to upper castes in colonial times has now been replaced with female foeticide with the extensive use of sex-selective technology across caste lines. Micro-level studies have shown that foeticide is practised across different caste groups to limit the family size with at least one son in the family (John et al., 2008). There are numerous reports in print and electronic media about killing or abandoning the girl child by the father or close family members.

Worldwide Sex Ratio Trends

The sex ratio trends of countries are as under:

Table 1

Sex Ratio Trends of Countries

S.No.	*Country*	*Census 2001*	*Census 2011*
1.	World	986	984
2.	China	944	926
3.	India	933	940
4.	USA	1,029	1,025
5.	Indonesia	1,004	988
6.	Brazil	1,025	1,042
7.	Pakistan	938	943
8.	Russian Fed.	1,140	1,167
9.	Bangladesh	958	978
10.	Japan	1,041	1,055
11.	Nigeria	1,016	987

Source: 2011 World Population Prospects revision 2008 UN.

The worldwide sex ratio shows diverse patterns across different countries of the world. The world sex ratio stands at 984 females against 1,000 males in 2011 Census. While in USA, Russian Federation, Japan and Brazil, females outnumber males, in the other six countries the balance is tilted towards the males. When compared to the previous decade, China, Indonesia, Nigeria and USA have shown a decline in the sex ratio in the present decade. The decline has been particularly sharp in Nigeria and Indonesia.

Sex Ratio Trends in India: An Overview

The sex ratio in India has been historically negative or in other words, unfavourable to females. In the pre-Independence period, the sex ratio declined consistently up to 1951 when it rose marginally. In the post-Independence period, the trend continued and the sex ratio slipped down for two consecutive decades after 1951 to reach 930 in 1971. During 1961–71, a steep fall of 11 points was seen in the sex ratio. The issue of unfavourable sex ratio in India is not a recent one; it gained the attention of colonial rulers during British time as well. The historical evidences of female infanticide and infant mortality in North and North–West India have been very well recorded (Agnihotri, 2000; Premi, 2001; Mitra, 2001; Vishwanath, 2004). In post-Independent India, the phenomenon was brought forward in late '60s and '70s by demographers, who witnessed a declining trend from the turn of 20th century onwards. The deficit of daughters, which was not evident in 1981, except in historically masculine states such as Punjab and Haryana, became quite evident by 2001 in states like Himachal Pradesh, Gujarat, Rajasthan, Madhya Pradesh and Maharashtra. It was in these states that private sex determination clinics were first

Table 2

Trends in Sex Ratio in India Since 1901

Year	*Sex Ratio (females per 1,000 males)*
1901	972
1911	964
1921	955
1931	950
1941	945
1951	946
1961	941
1971	930
1981	934
1991	927
2001	933
2011	940

Source: Census of India 2011.

established and the practice of selective abortion became popular from the late 1970s. Eminent demographer Ashish Bose (2001) coined an interesting term DEMARU (daughter elimination and male craze for ultrasound) and categorically remarked about Haryana as DEMARU or 'daughter maru' state. Desperation for male child is clearly seen in the mindset of the people. The table given below shows the continued skewed sex ratio in India since 1901.

Trends of Sex Ratio in States and UTs: 2001–2011

The patterns in sex ratio among the states and Union Territories are distinct. The top three states recording the highest overall sex ratio are neighbours located in the southern part of India, namely Kerala (1,084), Tamil Nadu (995), and Andhra Pradesh (992). Among the UTs, the top three are Puducherry (1,038), Lakshadweep (946) and the Andaman and Nicobar Islands (878). The lowest sex ratio among the states has been recorded in Haryana (877), Jammu and Kashmir (883) and Sikkim (889). Among the UTs, the lowest sex ratio has been recorded in Daman and Diu (618), Dadra and Nagar Haveli (775) and Chandigarh (818).

Table 3

Sex Ratio of Total Population and Child Population in the Age Group 0–6 and 7+ Years (2001 and 2011)

State/ UT Code	*India/ States/ Union Territory*	*Sex Ratio (females per 1,000 males)*					
		Total Population		*Child Population in the Age Group 0–6*		*Population Aged 7 and Above*	
		2001	*2011*	*2001*	*2011*	*2001*	*2011*
	India	933	940	927	914	934	944
01	Jammu & Kashmir	892	883	941	859	884	887
02	Himachal Pradesh	968	974	896	906	980	983
03	Punjab	876	893	789	846	888	899

Cont'd...

...Cont'd

04	Chandigarh	777	818	845	867	767	812
05	Uttarakhand	962	963	908	886	973	975
06	Haryana	861	877	819	830	869	885
07	NCT of Delhi	821	866	868	866	813	866
08	Rajasthan	921	926	909	883	923	935
09	Uttar Pradesh	898	908	916	899	894	910
10	Bihar	919	916	942	933	914	912
11	Sikkim	875	889	963	944	861	883
12	Arunachal Pradesh	893	920	964	960	878	913
13	Nagaland	900	931	964	944	890	929
14	Manipur	974	987	957	934	977	995
15	Mizoram	935	975	964	971	930	976
16	Tripura	948	961	966	953	945	962
17	Meghalaya	972	986	973	970	971	989
18	Assam	935	954	965	957	929	953
19	West Bengal	934	947	960	950	929	946
20	Jharkhand	941	947	965	943	935	948
21	Odisha	972	978	953	934	976	985
22	Chhattisgarh	989	991	975	964	992	995
23	Madhya Pradesh	919	930	932	912	916	933
24	Gujarat	920	918	883	886	927	923
25	Daman & Diu	710	618	926	909	682	589
26	Dadra & Nagar Haveli	812	775	979	924	779	752
27	Maharashtra	922	925	913	883	924	931
28	Andhra Pradesh	978	992	961	943	981	997
29	Karnataka	965	968	946	943	968	971
30	Goa	961	968	938	920	964	973
31	Lakshadweep	948	946	959	908	946	951
32	Kerala	1,058	1,084	960	959	1,072	1,099
33	Tamil Nadu	987	995	942	946	993	1,000
34	Puducherry	1,001	1,038	967	965	1,006	1,047

Source: Census of India 2001 and 2011.

Two major states, Bihar and Jammu and Kashmir, have shown a decline in the sex ratio. The other Union Territories registering a decline in overall sex ratio include Dadra and Nagar Haveli, Daman and Diu and Lakshadweep. Table 3 gives the recent trends of sex ratio of the total population, sex ratio in the age group 0–6 years and sex ratio of population aged 7 years and above for 2001 and 2011 for all the states and Union Territories.

Child Sex Ratio (0–6 Age Group)

While the overall sex ratio presents somewhat encouraging trends across the country; the same is not true in the case of the girl child in the age group of 0–6 years. There is a sharp decline in child sex ratio from 976 in 1961 Census to 914 in 2011 Census. This is evident from the table given below:

Table 4

Overall Sex Ratio and Child Sex Ratio from 1961–2011 Censuses

Year	*Overall Sex Ratio*	*Child Sex Ratio (0–6)*
1961	941	976
1971	930	964
1981	934	962
1991	927	945
2001	933	927
2011	940	914

Source: Census 2001 and 2011.

Inter-State Variations in Child Sex Ratio

Though there is improvement in the sex ratio of the total population nationwide as well as in most of the states, what is perplexing is the sharp declines observed in child sex ratio in North–Western states followed by Northern states, North–Eastern states and Eastern states while in Southern states, it declined moderately showing some optimism and favourable attitude towards the girl child. There are sharp inter-state variations in CSR. The lowest child sex ratios (0–6 years) among the states have been observed in the states of Haryana (830), Punjab (846) and Jammu and Kashmir (859) while among the UTs, Delhi (866), Chandigarh (867) and Lakshadweep (908) occupy the bottom position.

As regards the rising trend in CSR in Census 2011, child sex ratio (0–6 years) has registered an increasing trend only in six states and two UTs. What gives some cause for cheer is the fact that the states where the child sex ratio had dropped alarmingly in Census 2001 have now shown a slight improvement. This increase is substantial in Punjab (789 to 846 – 57 points), Haryana (819 to 830 – 11 points), Himachal Pradesh (896 to 906 – 10 points), Chandigarh (845 to 867 – 22 points), Gujarat (883 to 886 – 3 points) and Tamil Nadu (942 to 946 – 4 points). In addition, Mizoram (964 to 971 – 7 points) and Andaman and Nicobar Islands (957 to 966 – 9 points) have also shown an increasing trend in child sex ratio during 2001–2011.

At the same time, the situation in other states/UTs has been disconcerting. The child sex ratio (0–6 years) has declined in 27 states and Union Territories. The sharp fall in the range of 22 to 82 points have been reported in child sex ratios in Jammu and Kashmir (82), Dadra and Nagar Haveli, Lakshadweep, Maharashtra, Rajasthan, Manipur, Uttarakhand, Jharkhand, Madhya Pradesh and Nagaland during 2001–2011. It is to be noticed that even North–Eastern states like Sikkim and Arunachal Pradesh have shown a declining trend.

Bottom Ten Districts with Lowest Child Sex Ratio

Censuses 2001 and 2011 list the bottom ten districts with lowest child sex ratios. Some of the districts that had the lowest child sex ratio in 2001 Census gained in 2011 Census whereas some new districts such as Samba in Jammu and Kashmir and Beed in Maharashtra registered sharp declines in child sex ratio and were included in the list of bottom ten districts. The bottom ten districts with lowest CSR are as under:

Table 5

Bottom Ten Districts According to Child Sex Ratio (0–6 age group)

Census 2001			*Census 2011*		
District	*State*	*CSR*	*District*	*State*	*CSR*
Fatehgarh Sahib	Punjab	766	Jhajjar	Haryana	774
Patiala	Punjab	777	Mahendergarh	Haryana	778
Mansa	Punjab	782	Rewari	Haryana	784
Bathinda	Punjab	785	Samba	Jammu & Kashmir	787
Kapurthala	Punjab	785	Sonipat	Haryana	790
Sangrur	Punjab	786	Jammu	Jammu & Kashmir	794
Gurdaspur	Punjab	789	Beed	Maharashtra	800
Kurukshetra	Haryana	771	Ambala	Haryana	806
Ambala	Haryana	782	Rohtak	Haryana	807
Sonipat	Haryana	788	Pithoragarh	Uttarakhand	812

Source: Census of India, 2001 and 2011.

It shows that in 2001 Census, the bottom ten districts in CSR fall in the two prosperous states of Punjab and Haryana. In 2001 Census, Fatehgarh Sahib in Punjab had the lowest CSR (766). In 2011 Census, some new districts like Jhajjar in Haryana topped the list of lowest CSR followed by Mahendergarh and Rewari. In 2001 Census, these districts had the highest CSR. Samba in Jammu and Kashmir, Beed in Maharashtra and Pithoragarh in Uttarakhand joined the ranks of bottom ten districts.

Sex Ratio at Birth

Sex ratio at birth is an important indicator displaying the plight of the girl child. If we look at the sex ratio at birth, we find that at world level, the normal sex ratio at birth (SRB) is about 105 males per 100 females. The normal sex ratios at birth are found to lie between 943 and 971 females per 1,000 males. Accordingly, the normal figures for SRB are 953 females per 1,000 male children (Retherford and Roy, 2003; Arnold et al., 2002). In India, the normal SRB is worked out as female births per 1,000 males, which comes out to 950, i.e. a normal SRB. On the contrary, what is worrisome is the fact that the sex ratio at birth has been declining in India and many states and there are big gaps between male and female births. This is further substantiated by NFHS reports overtime shown in the table given below:

Table 6

Sex Ratio at Birth for the Major States

India and States	*NFHS–1 (92–93)*	*NFHS–2 (98–99)*	*NFHS–3 (05–06)*
India	951	935	920
Haryana	881	849	756
Punjab	876	860	728
Tamil Nadu	1,021	946	930
Kerala	1,010	929	902
Delhi	926	828	848

Source: National Family and Health Surveys–1, 11 and 111.

The NFHS-based sex ratios at birth show a sharp decline in SRB not only in India but other states as well except Delhi, where there is some increase in SRB in NFHS–3. Punjab has the lowest SRB (728), followed by Haryana and Maharashtra. Surprisingly, Kerala too has seen a consistent decline in SRB as indicated in NFHS reports.

Development Scenario and the Girl Child

India initiated certain fundamental economic reforms in 1990s. With relatively sustained high rates of growth during recent years, rapidly expanding private and service sectors, rising demand for well-educated professionals and a growing middle class, India is experiencing far-reaching consequences. These have either directly or indirectly increased the value attached to the acquisition of basic levels of information and knowledge. There is a general assumption that education, growing opportunities for productive work, particularly for women, and a consequent better standard of living would lead to more equal sex ratios but it does not seem to hold any significance in India's case. Above all, the big cities and towns with a high proportion of well-educated and prosperous citizens seem to refute this assumption. Paradoxically, the phenomenon appears to increase with development.

Economic development along with dissemination of ideas and technologies and increasing reach of the media has made a big impact on society, social values and aspirations. The coming together of small family norm, rising economic aspirations has resulted in the persistence of some age-old practices and the adoption of new practices, e.g. demand for more dowry at the time of marriage and continuing demand after marriage – including in-laws pressuring the girl to seek her share of parental property. Well-meaning and gender just laws have mutated with greater pressure on married women. Therefore, dowry and its manifestations continue for many years after marriage.

The overall socio-economic development in India particularly in North–West India in terms of better standard of living, improved health care specially maternal and infant and child health, increased life span, narrowed literacy level gaps between male and female, growing opportunities for work particularly for women have not resulted in equalizing sex ratios in general and gender relations in particular. Rather, the child sex ratio declines are not only getting worse but taking newer forms and manifestations. In this ongoing process of transformation, there is a trend towards smaller families where sons are favoured desperately, deselecting daughters at any cost. The economically developed states with higher per capita income have shown a decline in sex ratio. The economically developed states have better infrastructure, and are therefore in a better position to provide scientific technologies of sex selection, leading to a sharp decline in child sex ratio as evident from census information pertaining to child sex ratio in the developed states. Those familiar with the field situation in Punjab, Haryana, Himachal Pradesh, Chandigarh and Delhi know that the availability of doctors during the ultrasound test and consequent female foeticide, the good transportation network and the ability to pay for the services of the mobile doctors are factors responsible for the widespread recourse to ultrasound in rural areas also (Bose, 2001).

It shows that despite economic advancement of the society, the mindset of the people has not changed in favour of daughters. Rather, preference for 'son' is gaining all-time high momentum everywhere.

Family Planning Programme and Small Family Norm

India was the first among the few countries that initiated the Family Planning Programme along with the First Five Year Plan. The worldwide concern for population explosion was seriously considered by India's leaders and policy planners (Patel and Purewal, 2005). Moreover, overpopulation of India was taken as a deterrent for overall social and economic development of India. It was contended that to lead the nation on the path of development, reduce poverty and provide better quality of life to the people, reduction in the growth rate of population was essential. In order to control the growth rate of population, the family planning programme was launched vigorously emphasizing small family as an ideal family. Till late 1960s and early 1970s, the Family Planning Programme propagated a family size with 'two or three children', i.e. two sons and a daughter. Most of the highly educated urban-based families in cities and towns confined themselves to this 'ideal family size' with the help of contraception. This was the time when infant and child mortality was quite high, therefore a couple wanted to have two sons with a daughter. They did not want to take any chance and ensured that their children, particularly sons, survived and supported them in old age. In 1980s, the stress was laid on 'two child' family followed by 'one child' family in 1990s. During the past couple of years, there is a clear shift from the traditional to modern idea of small family size. Small family is considered an ideal family. Success of family planning programme can be seen by how seriously the message of two-child norm has articulated across different sections of society.

Along with it, India pioneered in legalizing abortions and right to abortion under certain conditions was legalized (MTP Act, 1971). Unlike women in the West, Indian women did not have to do much struggle to claim this right. Right to abortion in US was legalized in 1960s and its implementation took place much later. With the result, unwanted and unplanned pregnancies were being terminated under medical termination of pregnancies act (MTP Act, 1971) without having guilt whatsoever. In modern times, more and more medicalization of births, sonography and ultrasound checks have become common, resulting in sex selection, thus planning the families deliberately. One may ask a question that if family planning is important then why not planning the sex of children; why can't we leave it to people to decide the number and sex of children of their choice? The answer is not simple as it is located in the politics of commercialization of medicine and health care, state's role to control population and above all, the deep-rooted patriarchal social order where men are supreme and control their women and children. Women on the other hand are perceived as burdensome, less preferred and therefore denied the opportunities available to men. The idea of a 'balanced family' has a sexist bias. No one plans the family with a girl child. To have a daughter, no one has ever gone for ultrasound test and aborted the male child.

Son Preference and Sex-Selective Technology

Pre-natal sex selection is driven by an acute cultural ethos that favours the son and places low value on the daughter. Preference for 'son' has deep roots for socio-cultural and economic reasons in Indian society. Since daughters leave after marriage and become permanent members of in-laws' family, they are treated as 'outgoing' having little economic value. Sons on the other hand are counted as 'incoming' and permanent members of the family as they are supposed to support their ageing parents, continue family name and observe many rituals, particularly after-death rituals of parents in a patriarchal society. Investment on them is counted as important as it pays off. Several studies have revealed the strong desire to have sons among people across caste/class and community lines. Patrilocality, patrilineage and patriarchal attitudes exhibit women and girls having a lower position in the family, denial of property rights and low-paid jobs. Women's work such as cooking and cleaning is counted as 'no work' despite the fact that women work harder and for longer hours and contribute to economy, yet they are invisible and not counted as workers (Patel, 2003).

The birth of a son is perceived to be a symbol of upward mobility whereas the birth of a daughter is taken as a downward mobility. Though North India is the stronghold of extreme form of patriarchy where sons are desired desperately, it is now spreading to other parts of India too (ibid.). Eliminating girl child is the worst form of violence in human history. This is a gross violation of their rights to live in the society. It undermines their self-esteem and capacities to work and contribute for the society.

Pre-natal diagonostic techniques were introduced in India in early 1970s mainly for the detection of genetic abnormalities or metabolic disorders or chromosomal abnormalities or congenital malformations, or sex-linked disorders in the foetus. It was used to avoid pregnancies with abnormal growth of the foetus. Since 1994, the use of pre-natal diagnostic technique (PNDT) for other than medical purposes, i.e. sex determination is an offence, therefore illegal. The Pre-Natal Diagnostic Technique (PNDT) Act 1994 aims to regulate the use of PNDTs for medical purposes only to prevent its misuse for sex determination tests leading to female foeticide. Pre-natal diagnostic techniques basically refer to gynecological or obstetrical or medical procedures and techniques, taking or removing samples such as ultra sonography, foetoscopy amniotic fluids, chorionic villi, blood or any tissue of pregnant women sent to a genetic laboratory or genetic clinic. The PNDT Act 1994 came into force as a result of consistent efforts of women's struggle against the use of sex-selective technologies for sex determination leading to killing the female baby in the womb itself. Soon after PNDT, a new technology for pre-conception sex selection came to India through which the sex of the foetus could be decided well before conception by separating the X and Y chromosomes from sperms. To stop the misuse of this technology for sex determination, the PNDT Act was amended in 2002 and it was renamed as PCPNDT Act. This Act prohibits sex selection before/after the conception; any person, individual practitioners, centre or clinics, para-medical staff, Dai, ANM or Anganwadi worker found violating the Act will be convicted or imprisoned for a period of three years and can be fined ₹ 50,000. If found guilty, the registration of medical practitioner can be suspended or his/her name be removed from the register of council. Despite the monitoring system both at the state and Centre levels, the Act has been violated with impunity. Since sex determination and abortion of the foetus (if it is a female) are not linked while using the service, it becomes easier for both the parties to evade the law in connivance with service providers such as ultrasound and MTP.

As soon as the technology arrived in India in mid-'70s and people got to know that it is possible to ascertain the sex of the unborn child, it became popular for sex determination, leading to sex-selective abortions. People started using it to detect the sex of the foetus and plan the families, deciding the number of children as well as their sex composition. The termination of pregnancies was taking place not for reasons stated under MTP but to select sons while deselecting daughters. The technologies that help detect abnormalities in the unborn baby also help to identify the sex of the foetus so there is a thin line between the two and one's intention of using technology can only make the difference. The popularity of these tests became evident from the flourishing business in Delhi, Punjab, Haryana, Rajasthan, UP and other states. The first diagnostic centre was opened in Maharashtra for sex determination tests. After this, there was a mushrooming growth of several centres for sex determination all over India displaying hoardings that read: *'spend just ₹ 500 now or spend ₹ 50,000 later'*. In early 1979, the first sex determination centre was opened in Amritsar; soon, similar such clinics were opened in other parts of Punjab, Haryana, Uttar Pradesh, Rajasthan and Madhya Pradesh. In 2002, the Supreme Court passed strict strictures against the use of pre-natal diagnostic techniques for early sex detection and directed the state governments to impose a ban on such tests. Misuse of PNDT followed by sex-selective abortions has been observed to be an important factor for the skewed sex ratio at birth. Sociologists and demographers have often argued that sex selection takes place wherever there is a sharp fertility decline, with continued son preference and access to technologies and unregulated/illegal abortion services. Pre-natal sex selection is the worst form of gender discrimination. Of all the PNDTs, ultrasound known as 'sonography' is most commonly used and has become synonymous with the sex determination tests in India. Ultrasound is considered to provide the 'practical solution' to the 'problem' of girl children and one which obviates moral dilemmas. Sex-selective abortions are taken as a family planning method to limit the family size with at least one son in the family. Female foeticide is an extreme manifestation of poor status of women who are socially constructed inferior and less valuable sex and often projected as a burden on the family. Female foetuses are selectively aborted after pre-natal sex determination, thus avoiding the birth of girls. As a result of selective abortion, around 35 to 40 million girls are missing from the Indian population.

Several studies have categorically linked the relationship between low sex ratio and prosperity, pointing to the killing role of technology in enhancing the missing girl phenomena. This is quite evident that technology is facilitating 'sex-preference' leading to elimination of the girl children even before birth. Surprisingly, this trend is spreading all over India. So, what is happening now is that there is an unholy alliance between tradition (son complex) and technology which is playing havoc with the society at large (George and Dahiya, 1998; Premi, 2001; Bose, 2001; Agnihotri, 2000; Patel, 2007; Ahlawat, 2013). It is observed that the use of PNDT declines as the order of birth increases. The technology is misused particularly when the birth order is four or more and 40 per cent people resort to abortion if the foetus is female. Apparently, in the case of first birth, the predominant reason to use technology is the detection of abnormality in the foetus; at the higher orders of births, the main reason to use technology is to know about the sex of the foetus particularly if there is no son (Bhat and Xavier, 2007). A study (John et al., 2008) on 'Adverse Sex Ratio' conducted in Punjab and Haryana revealed a particular situation where affluent and educated households across caste lines use the sex-selective technologies particularly in second order birth onwards to plan the family size. Abortion is also accepted as the mode of limiting family size; enable spacing and regulating sex composition of the family. A woman from Punjab stated, 'Today's women do not have to make guesses. Ultrasound is the biggest of all guesses. You can get the clear report. Get your ultrasound done and you know what is there.' Here, ultrasound technology is explicitly sought for sex determination. The respondents from Punjab and Haryana admitted having undergone multiple abortions, sometimes as many as 6–8, after a daughter till she had a son – such examples abound and people know that sex-selective abortion is a crime. On female foeticide, a woman in Rohtak (rural) said, 'Till a male child is not born, killing female child is not a murder. If it is, then everyone is doing it. Now everyone gets a son by abortion only.' The major cause for decline in sex ratio is sex-selective foeticide (Sen, 2002). It is also observed and substantiated through census data that wherever female literacy improved, the child sex ratio declined (Chattopadhyay, 2003). The disadvantaged sex is less in numbers whether through infanticide or neglect or foeticide.

The commercialization of the medical profession as well as of human relations, large-scale publicity by mass media, small family norm particularly when cost of living is high and it is difficult to raise many children has really justified the use of sex-selective technologies leading to foeticide (Patel, 2007). There is a huge market with national and multinational companies investing in sex-selective technologies to make profit. Doctors, private practitioners and para-medical staff have considerable financial gains investing in ultrasound scanners (George and Dahiya, 1998). The popularity of sex pre-selection tests may even be higher than those of sex determination tests; these tests just do not involve any ethical issues related to elimination of female baby in the womb. Dr Ronald Erricsson has a chain of clinics conducting sex pre-selection tests in 46 countries in Europe, America, Asia and Latin America. He found that out of 263 couples who approached him for begetting a child, 248 aspired to have sons and only 15 selected daughters. This shows that preference for male child is not just limited to third world countries like India but it is spreading to developed countries too (Patel, 2003). Though scientists and medical practitioners deny any responsibility for the implications of these tests, it is important to raise a question regarding the value neutrality of science and technology. Basically, science and technology do not operate in vacuum; they are very much contextual and play an important role in shaping socio-cultural reality. China is one such example which despite having a revolution for 'socialist reconstruction' extensively used sex-selection technology to select male child after its government adopted the one-child family. It shows that the earlier practice of infanticide is replaced with foeticide. Female infanticide, female foeticide and abandonment of children are widely practised in contemporary society that is modern, technologically advanced and economically developed. Despite legislation, people defy laws to continue with socially acceptable norms.

Herbal Potions and Blessings of Holy Men to Ensure Son

Though there is little documentation on the role of herbal potions and prescriptions, there are significant evidences to show how vigorously such practices are prevalent among people across caste/class and religious lines. There is a wide prevalence of traditional healers all over India proclaiming the birth of male child even after two to three months of conception.

In December, 2005, a health fair known as Vindhiya Herbal Rashtriya Mela was organized by Madhya Pradesh government in Bhopal. In this fair, a large number of quacks and traditional healers practised under the banner of government and ensured 100 per cent guarantee of bearing male child through the use of concoctions. People were convinced that if they take '*Shivlingi seeds*' (herbal seeds) with cow's milk, sons will surely be born. '*Bachhi ke bachha bhi ho sakta hai*' (she-calf can produce he-calf), emphasized a traditional healer. In another study (2008) conducted in Punjab and Haryana on 'Adverse Sex Ratio,' it was observed that desperation for son is so high that people in these two states visit '*deras*' and '*samadhs*' (holy places) where herbal potions and remedies are given to women to ensure male child. It was observed that young women are taken to such places immediately after marriage in the name of seeking blessings of holy men and offer prayers accompanied by mother, mother-in-law, husband, sister-in-law, etc. There are many cases of couples across caste and class lines using 'herbal potions' to confirm male child right at the time of first conception and later on abort if it is a female foetus. It has been reported that in a large number of women who had taken such potions, the pregnancy culminated into miscarriages or still-births or in some cases children were born with defects. Desire for son is so intense that despite congenital defects, nothing is stopping people from using these potions to have male child. Even if couples have availed of herbal potions/blessings of holy men, surety is guaranteed only by ultrasound (John et al., 2008).

Non-Marriage of Men

Scarcity of brides in contemporary Punjab and Haryana is a serious implication of skewed child sex ratio, leading to non-marriage of young men. Since girls are already lesser in number and better educated, therefore families look for better placed boys, preferably urban, resulting in squeezing of marriage cohort (Ahlawat, 2009). No one would like to marry his/her daughter to a person who does not earn for himself and the family. One of the serious implications of the skewed sex ratio is reflected in 'male marriage squeeze'. To cope with the situation, men across caste lines are bringing brides from distant states like Uttarakhand, Bihar, Jharkhand, West Bengal, Maharashtra, North–East and even Kerala. These women are brought from across cultural, regional and language contexts where caste and sometimes even religion is different (Kaur, 2004; Ahlawat, 2012, 2015).

State Initiatives and the Girl Child

In order to protect the girl child and improve her status in the society, various schemes and programmes have been implemented at central as well as at state levels. Besides the newly-launched schemes, there are some old ongoing programmes such as Integrated Child Development Scheme (ICDS), which is run through Anganwadi centres for pre-school children as well as pregnant and lactating mothers. The new schemes such as 'Kanya Dan Scheme', 'Apni Beti Apna Dhan', 'Balika Samridhi Yojana', 'Shagun', 'Ladli', monitoring of pregnancies in district with low sex ratio, cradle scheme are some of the important schemes launched by the Department of Women and Child Development to raise the value of the girl child, to check infanticide and sex-selective abortions, thereby improving the sex ratio in general and the plight of girl child in particular.

Despite Central and state government initiatives in the form of various schemes and programmes to strengthen the girl child, enactment of PCPNDT Act (1994, amended 2003) to check the unscrupulous use of sex determination technologies, role of media to sensitize the society at large and reporting on girl child deficit and sustained efforts and campaign of civil society organizations and activists, nothing seems to be working to stop discrimination against the girl child. Rather the nexus among doctors, nurses, ANMs and other medical, para-medical personnel is flourishing into big business deals. On the contrary, Planning Commission's proposal for relaxing the ban on sex determination tests is a regressive move, made in the name of 'flexibility and choice' tantamount to accepting the argument that sex selection is a matter of 'freedom of choice', which has already been struck down by the courts while upholding the PC and PNDT Act. However, both the 2001 and the 2011 Census reports have clearly shown that the implementation of the Act has been tardy as there has been a further decline in child sex ratio. Planning Commission's move will only encourage the virtual abandonment of a large number of girl children. It is well known that conditions of most orphanages and remand homes are insecure and deplorable, and innumerable cases of physical and sexual abuse, trafficking, etc., have come to light. The solution is not to 'incentivize' the adoption of female foetuses, but to encourage the birth of girls with a slew of economic and social measures that will help to root out the discrimination faced by them.

Looking Beyond

It is time to create awareness among different stakeholders and the community at large about the negative impact of declining child sex ratio on society. State intervention is needed to strictly regulate pre-conception/pre-natal technologies and to prevent import of newer at-home sex determination technologies. It is equally important to break the nexus between ANMs and local para-medical staff, radiologists and medical practitioners.

It is equally important to empower women to create gender just society. Women too should come forward and take the responsibility of their ageing parents to reduce parents' dependence on sons. There is need to create a support structure through market or state to provide quality care to ageing people in the society. Religious leaders have a great role to play by discouraging discrimination against the girl child and female foeticide.

About the Book

The papers in this volume attempt to cover multiplex dimensions related to the girl child. Social and economic development, cultural dimensions, affluence, educational levels, urban residence and exposure of media both print and electronic have made a tremendous impact on the society. Use as well as misuse of sex-selective technologies is a new dimension that has both helped in detecting the abnormalities or defects in unborn baby and at the same time have been playing havoc with the already declining sex ratio in general and child sex ratio in particular. The contributors in this book have focused on multi-layered dimensions influencing the child sex ratio and the girl child in the Indian context.

Virinder Singh's paper on 'Destruction and Denial of Motherhood: Where to Search for the Paradoxes' questions the very model of development full of paradoxes; the way it is conceived; the way it is planned; the way it is projected and the nature of its effects is all paradoxical. The processes associated with development like growth, GNP, increase in productivity, globalization and liberalization have been projected as panacea for the solution to the problems. This has become a new pantheon of gods, to be worshipped to solve all the problems. In such a situation, do we expect anything different in case of infanticide and foeticide and more particularly female infanticide and female foeticide? When daughters are objectified as sources of transfer of wealth and property, they become targets of hatred. These objectified daughters are feared because of their potential to upset property relations.

Mary John's paper on 'Child Sex Ratios and Gender Discrimination: Challenges for Law and Policy' raises certain important issues and complexities with regard to sex ratio phenomena at all-India level, particularly in North–West India. She argues that on one hand there is huge disenchantment with agriculture in this region, supplemented by highly volatile socio-economic forms of development. At the same time, modern changes are palpable – such as increase in educational attainments, and rise in the age of marriage leading to unintended consequences of contemporary social processes, compounding the sense of burden represented by the birth of a daughter. She also argues that there has been an invisible structural imbalance at work in most parts of the country outside the North–West, but which was never considered to be a problem to be 'corrected'. In most of the discussion on fertility and sex ratios, little attention is given to what is arguably the most critical indicator of the status of gender in our country. Surely, the government has to show greater political will in exposing the nexus between medical practitioners and the political machinery, if the law against sex selection is to have any chance of making sex selection a crime. But, unless both government and society acknowledge how 'choices' for having a girl are at the confluence of policies relating to access to health, education, sexual safety and economic viability, it is unlikely that we will see any lasting impact on the sex ratio, much less curtail its further spread.

Anjali Radkar in her paper 'Eliminating Daughters: An Unfortunate Reality of West and North–West India' has explained the age-old preference for sons over daughters. Son preference in India is universal and ancient. It actually is an indicator of social development. It portrays the social inequality and lower status of women in the society. The preference is influenced by various socio-economic and cultural factors. It is mainly the reflection of the wide gap in the differentials of roles of girls and boys. Looking at cost-benefits, sons are always valued more than daughters. In this context, they are considered as assets and daughters as liability. Actually, having a son is looked upon as a package for successful, smooth life rather than a single isolated cause. Along with the lineage and old-age support, the psychological satisfaction of having a son and inner need to feel complete are the causes of desire for sons.

Neerja Ahlawat's paper on 'Eliminating Daughters and Selecting Sons: Planning Families' highlights that the overall sex ratio at national level (the number of females per 1,000 males) has improved by seven points from 933 in 2001 Census to 940 in 2011 Census. However, the matter of concern is the lowest child sex ratio of 914 girls per 1,000 boys at national level in 2011 Census as against 927 in 2001 Census. It shows that aversion to daughters continues despite PCPNDT Act and state measures to protect the girl child. This paper examines how the family plans and uses discrete strategies to limit the family size, deciding the number of children particularly sons and daughters in the family. Why daughters have always been dispensed with and sons though considered essential but their number in the family is again not unlimited? Deficit in girl child population is leading to 'male marriage squeeze', a serious implication of the shortage of marriageable age girls.

Manjeet Rathee's paper on 'Women and the Conservative Backlash in Society and Media' discusses the discriminatory and violent practice of female infanticide due to subordinate status of women that has long existed in Indian society, but has acquired new dimensions in the present conditions when the paradigm of 'development' and 'new technology' is being used for 'civilized' extermination of a particular sex and that too in the name of 'democratic choice', leading not only to pre-birth killing of millions of girl children but a terrible imbalance in the male-female ratio. The steep fall in the child sex ratio – the lowest since Independence – is a crude indictment of the policies of the Central and state governments and an exposure of its utter failure to implement the PCPNDT Act. The paper attempts to bring to the fore the emerging trends of this inhuman practice reflected in Haryana in the form of changing nature of violence through new ways of dowry and marriage, including 'bought wives' from other states, erosion of human values at the level of inter-personal relationships, the horror of 'honour killings' and diktats by traditional caste panchayats against choice marriages. Based on field work experiences conducted in Haryana, and the role of state government, the paper attempts to suggest certain immediate interventions.

Anjali Dewan's paper on 'Dispensing with Daughters: Exploring the Socio-Economic and Cultural Dimensions of Female Foeticide and Infanticide' highlights that cultural and economic factors lead to female infanticide and sex-selective abortions. The practice of dowry has made women/girls to be a liability. They believe that girls' education does not add to the income of the girls' family. The socio-economic pressures favouring sons are so strong that women undergo female foeticide despite possible health problems resulting from an abortion and their belief that abortion is a sin. Legislation prohibiting the use of pre-natal diagnostic tests to determine the sex of the foetus does not solve this problem. Improving women's status in society will reduce social prejudices which, in turn, will decrease female foeticide. The present paper deals with an analysis of incidence of foeticide, infanticide, the causes, intervention steps taken by the government and the remedial measures to eliminate the menace.

Dweepika Kumari in her paper on 'Behavioural Categorization of Women Based on Empowerment Level and the Extent of Son-Preference: A Case Study of Patna' aims to discuss that Indian women are generally considered to be quite traditional having a strong son/male preference and belief in the established customs. They also tend to impart these traditional values to their daughters and daughters- in-law. The young women, who are thus conditioned from their very childhood to be meek and docile, lose their self-confidence and always silently submit to whatever is imposed on them. The increasing level of education has increased their level of confidence and makes their views independent but they too remain socially conditioned and often compromise their own ideologies just to satisfy the family. The present paper is based on the findings of a primary survey and empirical observations and attempts at grouping the women into distinct behavioural categories. This categorization can prove to be helpful in formulating different plans and policies for different categories of women in dealing with the problem of excessive son preference in Indian families.

Jaya Kritika Ojha and Binod Mishra's joint paper on 'Ensuring Dignity of the Girl Child: A Case Study of URMUL Initiative in Sri Ganganagar District of Rajasthan' shows the proactive approach of the organization in raising the value of the girl child. Realizing the challenging issue of female foeticide, URMUL took the social responsibility to work against girl child discrimination through awareness generation projects to stop female foeticide. URMUL's efforts and interventions have made a positive change in people's attitudes towards the girl child in Rajasthan.

Mitu Khurana in her paper on 'Combating Female Foeticide: PCPNDT Act and Its Implementation' examines the actions taken against the guilty under the PCPNDT Act by the implementing authorities (i.e. the Chief District Medical Officer–CDMO) in Delhi.

Sudha Yadav's paper on 'Female Foeticide: A Silent Violence' discusses female foeticide as a unique form of violence against women and the girl child. Female infanticide has always been in practice in our country since times immemorial. This has been replaced by foeticide and is fast spreading to less developed regions both in rural as well as urban areas. Preference for the male child is so intense that sex-selective technologies are used to eliminate the girl child. The paper deals with the analysis of incidence of foeticide, its causes and consequences, legislative actions taken by the government and the remedial measures to eliminate the menace.

Sonu Dehmiwal's paper on 'Girl Child Discrimination Since Conception of Life: Role of Laws and Government Policies' discusses the socio-economic and cultural practices responsible for discrimination against the girl child. She highlights the legal framework to deal with the emerging issues related with the protection of the girl child. She argues that there should be strong implementation of PCPNDT Act as well as policies to protect and promote the girl child. But most importantly, the solution lies in enhancing the status of women through empowerment.

References

Agnihotri, Satish Balram. 2000. *Sex Ratio Patterns in the Indian Population: A Fresh Exploration*, New Delhi: Sage Publications.

Ahlawat, N. 2009. 'Missing Brides in Rural Haryana', *Social Change*, Vol. 39, No. 1, March.

— 2012. 'Political Economy of Haryana's Khaps', *Economic and Political Weekly*, Volume XLV11, No. 47–48, December 01.

— 2013. 'Dispensable Daughters and Indispensable Sons', *Social Change*, 43(3) pp. 365–376.

— 2015. 'Marriage Norms, Personal Choices and Social Sanctions in Haryana', *Sociological Bulletin*, Volume 64, No. 1, January–April.

Bhat, P.N. Mari and A.J. Francis Zavier. 2007. 'Factors Influencing the Use of Prenatal Diagnostic Techniques and the Sex Ratio at Birth', *Economic and Political Weekly*, Vol. XLII, No. 24, 16–22 June.

Bose, A. 2001. *India's Billion Plus People: 2001 Census Highlights, Methodology and Media Coverage*, New Delhi: B.R. Publishing Corporation.

Brown, John Cave. 1857. *Indian Infanticide: Its Origin, Progress and Suppression*, London: W.H. Allen.

Census of India. 2001 and 2011. Population Tables, Census of India, Office of Registrar General, India, Ministry of Home Affairs, Government of India, New Delhi.

Chattopadhyay, D. 2003. 'Child Sex Ratio on the Decline in Bengal Report', *The Times of India*, Mumbai, 10 March.

Dasgupta, M. 1987. 'Selective Discrimination Against Female Children in Rural Punjab', *Population and Development Review*, Vol. 13, No. 1, pp. 77–100.

Dreze, Jean and Amartya Sen. 1975. *India: Economic Development and Social Opportunity*, Delhi: Oxford University Press.

Dyson, Tim and Mick Moore. 1983. 'On Kinship Structure, Female Autonomy and Demographic Behaviour in India', *Population and Development Review*, Vol. 9, No. 1, pp. 35–60.

George, S. and R. Dahiya. 1998. 'Female Foeticide in Rural Haryana', *Economic and Political Weekly*, Vol. XXXIII, No. 32, pp. 2191–98.

John, Mary E., Ravinder Kaur, Rajni Palriwala, Saraswati Raju and Alpana Sagar. 2008. *Planning Families, Planning Gender: The Adverse Child Sex Ratio in Selected Districts of Punjab, Haryana, Himachal Pradesh, Rajasthan and Madhya Pradesh*, Bangalore: Books for Change.

Kaur, R. 2004. 'Across Region Marriages: Poverty, Female Migration and Sex Ratio', *Economic and Political Weekly*, Vol. XXXIX, No. 25.

Kaye, John. 1966. *The Administration of East India Company*, Allahabad: Kitab Mahal Pvt. Ltd. (Reprint).

Kishor, Sunita. 1995. 'Gender Differentials in Child Mortality: A Review of Evidence', in Monica Dasgupta, Lincoln C. Chen and T.N. Krishnan (eds), *Women's Health in India: Risk and Vulnerability*, Bombay: Oxford University Press, pp. 19–54.

Kynch, J. and A. Sen. 1983. 'Indian Women: Well-Being and Survival', *Cambridge Journal of Economics*, Vol. 7, No. 3, pp. 363–80.

Mahadevan, K. 1979. *Sociology of Fertility: Determinants of Fertility Differentials in South India*, New Delhi: Sterling Publishers.

Miller, B. 1981. *The Endangered Sex: Neglect of Female Children in Rural North India*, Ithaca, NY: Cornell University Press.

——. 1987. 'Female Infanticide and Child Neglect in Rural North India', in Nancy Scheper-Hughes (ed.), *Child Survival*, Thousand Oaks, CA: Sage Publications.

——. 1989. 'Changing Patterns of Juvenile Sex Ratios in Rural India, 1961–1971', *Economic and Political Weekly*, Vol. 20, No. 2, 2 June, pp. 1229–36.

Mitra, Ashok. 2001. 'Implications of Declining Sex Ratio in India's Population', in Vina Mazumdar and N. Krishnaji (eds), *Enduring Conundrum: India's Sex Ratio*, Delhi: Rainbow Publishers, pp. 149–98.

National Health and Family Surveys 1, 11 and 111.

Pakrasi, K. 1970. 'Infanticide: Vital Statistics and Proclaimed Castes of India', *Sociological Bulletin*, No. 2, pp. 81–98.

Patel, T. 2007. 'Female Foeticide, Family Planning and State-Society in India', in Tulsi Patel (ed.), *Sex Selective Abortion in India: Gender, Society and New Reproductive Technologies*, New Delhi: Sage Publications, pp. 316–56.

Patel, T. and T. Purewal. 2005. 'Inequality, Population Politics and NGOs', in M. Romerao and E. Margolis (eds), *The Blackwell Companion to Social Inequality*, New York: Blackwell, pp. 441–65.

Patel, V. 2003. 'The Girl Child: Health Status in Post-Independence Period', *The National Medical Journal of India*, Vol. 16, No. 2, pp. 42–45.

Premi, M.K. and S. Raju. 1996. 'Imbalance in Child Sex Ratio in Madhya Pradesh, Unpublished Report', Sponsored by Ministry of Human Resource Development, Government of India.

Premi, M.K. 2001. 'The Missing Girl Child', *Economic and Political eekly*, Vol. 36, No. 21, pp. 1875–80.

Rajaretnam, T. 1992. 'Female Infanticide Among Pramalal Kallars in Tamil Nadu', *Social Change*, Vol. 22, No. 3, pp. 107–10.

Retherford, Robert D. and T.K. Roy. 2003. 'Factors Affecting Sex Selective Abortions in 17 Major States', National Family Health Survey Reports, Number 21, International Institute for Population Sciences, Mumbai, India, East-West Center Program on Population, Honolulu, Hawaii, USA.

Sen, Amartya. 1990. 'More than 100 Million Women are Missing', *New York Review of Books*, Vol. 37, No. 20, December.

Sen, V. 2002. '2001 Census of India: Report for Kolkata', Director of Census Operations, West Bengal.

Sudha, S. and S. Irudaya Rajan. 1999. 'Female Demographic Disadvantage in India, 1991: Sex Selective Abortions and Female Infanticide, 1981–1991', *Development and Change*, Vol. 30, No. 2, pp. 585–61.

Venkataramani, S.H. 1986. 'Born to Die: Female Infanticide', *India Today*, 15 June, pp. 26–33.

Visaria, P. 1971. *The Sex Ratio of the Population of India*, Census of India 1961, Monograph No. 10, Office of the Registrar General, India.

Vishwanath, I.S. 2004. 'Female Infanticide: The Colonial Experience', *Economic and Political Weekly*, 29 May.

1

Destruction and Denial of Motherhood

Where to Search for the Paradoxes

Virinder Singh

Do we expect development to be without paradoxes? Rather, the nature of development we have is full of paradoxes. The way it is conceived, the way it is planned, the way it is projected and the nature of its effects is all paradoxical. The processes associated with development like growth, GNP, increase in productivity, globalization and liberalization have been projected as panacea for the problems. This has become a new pantheon of gods, to be worshipped to solve all our problems. The greed and acquisition of more and more wealth have become sacred practices. Our expectations are that all this will solve all our problems. If we do not have the fulfillment of our wishes, we consider it a paradox and also something surprising. In such a situation, it is not surprising that our frustrated hopes start the search for the paradoxes. It is not paradoxical at all, but it is normal. What is paradoxical? Our expectations that capitalist development is without paradoxes. Paradoxical is our expectation that all is well when greed-based and property crazy mindsets rule the minds of everybody. Do we believe that economic development takes care of all ethical issues? In an atmosphere where the sinister forces of greed and acquisition have a free play, everything else operates within limits set by these forces. In several cases, these forces consolidate the tensions and conflicts. In the competitive democratic system, the tradition is also mobilized and consolidated. The consolidation of the property-based crimes also takes place. Can we expect any thing different in case of infanticide and foeticide and more particularly female infanticide and female foeticide? When daughters are objectified as sources of transfer of wealth and property, they become targets of hate. These objectified daughters are feared because of their potential to upset property relations. The transfer of property accompanies woman to her in-laws' home.

The destruction of the offspring of all the creatures has been part of the process of natural selection as operative through the forces for the competition of resources. It is true for both intra and inter species competition. In these competitions, environmental factors have played key and decisive roles. This has led to local and global extinctions of several species. However, there is underlying unity in the behaviour of offsprings. The killings of the offspring by the parents are almost nonexistent. However, this is reflected in the behaviour of human parents without any instinctual restraints. This is something unique in the humans and this uniqueness is expressed in infanticide and foeticide.

While foeticide and its recent reflections in the gender-based foeticide is relatively a recent phenomenon, infanticide has been widely practised by most societies in history. It is one of the common threads which united humanity in past. This barbarous practice has been a fact in spite of our claimed superiority over non-humans. We are never tired of calling them brutes. Let's have a brief overview of the human brutishness in human history. Infanticide in history has been widespread; it was practised by various methods. Humans have been very inventive in this regard. Exposure of the unwanted infants was the most common method of getting rid of the extra burden. The infants were generally exposed in the forests where these were eaten by the wild animals or they died of hunger. Romans threw infants in Tiber. In ancient Rome, the un-wantedness of the infant was decided by fathers or pater familias. Some 'cultured' people put ashes in the mouths of infants and as a consequence they died of suffocation. Eskimos exposed the infants on ice to die. Even sacrifice of infants was widespread but it was not common. The killing of the infants was practised by both 'barbarians' and the 'civilized' and with equal ruthlessness. In some societies, it was planned and involved 10 to 15 per cent of the infants. In others, it was up to 50 per cent. The main and dominant sections did not allow this 'barbarous' practice. However, it continued unabated. In history, infanticide was openly advocated in the circumstances where resources were scarce and it was not possible to take the burden of extra child. It indirectly kept population under control. In some societies, infanticide was the direct policy matter to control the population. Abipones of Paraguay never reared more than two children.

These days, the practice of infanticide appears to be unethical to some educated sections of society. But in the past, it was never considered 'outrageous' by any civilization. The earlier ethical standards were shaped by the compulsions of those times. However, most of the times, the infants of both the sexes were treated equally. Some societies were even compassionate to female infants. The Romans rescued the abandoned female infants from the garbage dumps and reared them as highly skilled prostitutes. In some parts of India, female infants before killing were offered as future brides to the needy. There have been recent cases where male infants have been killed and females protected. To stop a long drawn war in Papua New Guinea, mothers started killing male infants to stop the future availability of soldiers. However, this seems to be an exception.

There have been famous philosophers (we may call them notorious) who advocated the killing of female infants. Gendricide was openly advocated by Chinese philosopher Han Fei Tzu in third century BC. He said, 'As to children, a father and mother, when they produce a boy, congratulate one and other but when they produce a girl, they put it to death.' In India, there has been no known philosopher advocating such ideas, but the situation has been no different than China. The celebrations of the birth of male child at the time in North–West India are a reminder of an inherent bias in favour of male child. While in India parents killed the new-born female infants and then buried them, the Chinese drowned the female infants in a bucket full of water. Some Red Indian tribes of USA indulged in female infanticide to such extremes that they had to procure brides from other tribes, a phenomenon no different than present day North–West India. Technology and foeticide and the growth of birth control technology in the form of abortions have made possible the destruction of embryo. This created controversy in its initial stages and still continues. This has been further complicated by the position of those who want to promote abortions as the right of the potential mothers to have or not to have a child. However, the practice of gender-based foeticide by the use of ultrasonic technology has created fresh problems. The scale at which the selective destruction of female foetus is being practised is alarming. The birth control technology and the rights are being openly misused for foetus-based gendricide, which has serious social and biological implications.[1] Some of these are described below.

Social and Biological Implications: Infanticide and foeticide have many implications. The most important is denial of fatherhood and motherhood to the parents. These 'denials' may be voluntary or forced. Voluntarily accepted family welfare programmes lead to such 'voluntary denials'. If these programmes are accepted under social and family pressures, these become 'forced denials'. The implications of these denials may be different for parents than for the society. These may be different for different parents. In a way infanticide practised due to the pressure of the scarcity of available resources was 'forced denial'. These denials of parenthood constitute the destruction of potential motherhood or fatherhood for the killed infants and aborted foetuses. This reflects the conflict between the interests of different generations. This may or if I am not wrong must generate an inter-generational ethical debate.

However, the problem becomes serious in case of selective and gender-based infanticide and foeticide or gendricide. As in the above case, this also leads to the denial of motherhood and fatherhood to the parents. But these denials of parenthood are gender-based. It does not destroy motherhood of a living mother as she can be the mother of a male child but destroys the potential motherhood of aborted female foetus and the female infant. The destruction of future mothers or the missing mothers of future shall have serious implications for the society. Immediately, it may be reflected in the truncated sex ratios as shown by various statistics. These statistics may be a warning sign and therefore fearful. But more fearful is the social deformation and social dislocation which must result from this truncated sex ratio.

If female foeticide and female infanticide remain confined to a region, this may adversely affect the local availability of brides (this is already happening in Haryana). The chronic shortage of brides encourages the procurement of brides from outside. This is mostly for a price. It is a form of traffic generally forbidden by law. But marriage as money or resource-mediated relation continues though with an important difference that instead of receiving dowry, bride price is paid. It throws up a challenge before caste and religion-based matrimonial relations with all the moral implications.

If the phenomenon of female foeticide and female infanticide becomes universal as it is likely to be in near future (though there is no immediate threat), then there shall be everywhere the general shortage of brides. Society shall have a large number of unmarried males chasing too few potential brides. The almost violent behaviour of these males inside the family and outside the family shall surely pose several moral issues. It shall be interesting to know how the society reacts to these ethical challenges of future. The family tensions based on the relationship of 'this woman's husband and that woman's son' shall be substituted by the tensions based on 'that man's wife and this man's mother'. In short, daughter-in-law and mother-in-law conflict is likely to be replaced by father and son conflict. How Hamlet and Oedipus behave in such a situation and how the society responds to it shall be an interesting topic for future discussion.

However, we must consider what normally happens in the society where everything is inspired by greed and possessive individualism, if people do not have daughters simply to avoid the transfer of large part of property in form of dowry to her in-laws. The possessive zeal is understandable. But the paradox associated with the payment of bride price which involves the transfer of resources to bride's family from which she is purchased is a double loss. The man loses the chance of getting dowry, which he would have got in case of marriage to a local girl. So the net outcome of such practices is negative. In the long run, the access to procured brides shall be definitely better for those having more resources. In such a situation where the commodification of brides takes place, the laws of market operate and the highest bidder shall have the access to the brides and therefore to sex. In the medieval times, the access to power led to more access to sexual resources. '*Harem*' was the symbol of power. Now it shall be the moneyed class which shall control the female sexual resources. The tensions associated with sharing of resources shall get associated with sex in its new forms.

These are the impending developments where we should look for the paradoxes. The economic development as understood in the capitalist society creates more problems than it is able to solve. The forces of liberalization, innovation are never oriented to solve social problems. These forces with their obsession with growth, GNP, etc., only further complicate the problems. All the claims of capitalism are paradoxical. It first removes forests then advocates tree plantation; it produces cars in large numbers and then widens roads; it first creates products then searches for the consumers; it first impoverishes people and then runs poverty alleviation programmes; it produces food in large quantities, allows it rot but shall not distribute it to the needy. Similarly, it produces conditions which are conducive to the commodification of family relations, which lead to gender-based discrimination and female foeticide and infanticide. Then it tries to provide incentives to protect female infants. But so far as all these negative and positive measures help to increase GNP, it is always welcome. The production of control or accentuate ultrasound machines adds to GNP, so also the services to control foeticide and infanticides. This is where the paradox of capitalist development lies. We should see the elimination of daughters in this context. So long as the greed-based property-loving society exists, there is no chance for survival of any thing which has a negative monetary value.

Possessive individualism and possessive family life of the extreme kind shall not allow an alternative perspective to emerge so easily. And this shall have serious implications for the emergence of the possible solution to the problems. This necessitates the transformation of property relations and the prevalence, rather domination, of greed in the society.[2] A greed-based society feeds on the weakness of people for the new demands, which are mostly surplus demands and have been created without taking into consideration their needs. This in turn creates an artificial need for the control of more resources and establishes the social relations based on property and possessions. The conjugal relations between the sexes are dominated by possessions and money. This alienation of sexual life is based upon the mediations established by possessions and private property. The concepts of handsomeness and beauty are transformed due to these mediations. Handsome is he who has a handsome job or bank balance. Similarly, beauty depends upon the potential of dowry. The solution for these problems cannot be found in the society or the system which sanctifies, preserves and promotes private property and possessions. The solution lies outside it. The existing private property relations stand in the way of a permanent solution to the problem. It is necessary to promote need-based ethos in place of greed-based ethos.

There is a strong inclination to search for solutions in science and technology. This is totally misconceived. The image of science and technology as holy cows has been created to provide false hopes to the victims of the society based upon private property and possessions. Ultrasonic machine has been invented to check the problems related to health; however, it earns a lot of money for the medical professionals with pre-natal testing of the sex of the foetus. There is a sinister alliance of the scientists, technologists, pharmaceutical industry and the policy planners. The elimination of female foeticide is not their concern but control over societal resources and profits is the major obsession. This is possible with continuation of the problem and if not, this something else can give them the same benefits. The obsession is with the lucrative business. It may be with HIV AIDS or pre-natal elimination of female foetuses. The obsession of NGOs with these problems is also limited by their financial needs and dependent on the funding agencies that make their fundamentals clear to them. But all this is part of the greed-based society which worships GNP. Science and technology are hopeless hope-givers; these create more problems than providing solutions. One solution provided by them is the foundation of hundreds of problems. This is due to their nature to find out piecemeal solutions to the problems understood in isolation. Added to it are the needs of survival as a profession which subordinates its interests to greed-based society. All this and several other reasons rule out any technological solutions to the problem of female foeticide.

If we do not have technological solutions to the problem of female foeticide and large sections of society are not yet ready for the radical transformation of relations based upon private property, possessions and mediations by money, then we should be ready to face serious consequences. Some of the consequences shall be:

1. The emergence of a strong force of sister-less brothers, who are less likely to respect the traditional ethos associated with sisterhood and brotherhood.
2. The strong social presence of emotionally imbalanced daughter-less fathers. They will not realize that the situation is their own creation.
3. Streets full of whistling bride-less bachelors, who shall be not only lawless but also a moral challenge to the society. The possibility of sex-based crimes and associated violence shall increase with the unforeseen consequences.
4. The chronic decrease in the number of brides shall increase their bargaining power and they might start asking for the bride price. However, this shall not change the basic nature of the private property and possession-based society. It shall lead to a different type of consolidation of same morality.
5. Associated with this is the strong likelihood of the emergence of Amazon dominated pockets at some places which might witness the prevalence of an entirely new morality.
6. It can be concluded from the scenario that with the shortage of possible brides and increase in their bargaining power, they shall definitely like to marry the highest bidder. This shall be the re-emergence of medieval practices in its latest form. With wealth chasing sex, the possibility of break-ups shall increase, adding to the existing uncertainty in social relations. Is the society ready to accept these changes in future. Maybe yes. But what shall be the consequences of this adjustment? This shall not be a minor cultural shock but a historical social earthquake. An earthquake which shakes the greed-based societies and transforms private property and possession-basedties; and money mediated

shall send pleasant tremors and provide solutions to most of evils of contemporary society.

7. However, the present situation is likely to continue in the foreseeable future. There is immediate or serious challenge to the greed-based outlook or the private property-based social relations. There are several other possibilities which may emerge in the future and above listing of the possibilities is only suggestive and not exhaustive.

For now, the commodification of the sexes and the associated problems like dowry shall not only continue but are likely to increase. Therefore, all the 'stakeholders' – the NGOs, government departments, the corporate sector, particularly multinationals, the press with paid news – should rest assured that their interests shall be secure so long as the problem of declining sex ratio of girls continue. The funds shall not only continue to flow but are likely to increase. As in the case of tiger conservation, lesser the tigers more the flow of funds for their conservation. In this case, lesser the girls, more shall be the availability of funds to stop female microbicide. In the initial stages, the problem attracted the 'stakeholders', and now the 'stakeholders' shall see to it that the problem not only continues but aggravates and shall ensure the continuous flow of funds. For this, newspaper reports, seminars, conferences, surveys, churning of data, government statements, steering committees, task forces shall be necessary. This shall be business as usual. It shall become a menace if you challenge the greed-based ethos of the existing institutions. If you do that, the wrath of the state accompanied by the lies of the corporate press and electronic news media shall be at full play. The solution to the problems is not very easy. This is the real paradox which needs to be understood and resolved. This was a very humble attempt at developing an alternative perspective to understand the problem and suggest limits of action in the contemporary situation and alternative options.

Notes

1. Extensive discussion about female foeticide based on the census and other data exists. However, by itself, this data is insufficient to explain the moral dilemma before the society. The explanations cannot be adequate by merely taking into consideration faceless number of missing girls or the cases of female foeticide. It needs to be recognized as an existential problem which has been compounded by the degenerate social situation. This problem defies easy solutions.
2. Possessive individualism is the term which was used by C.B. Macpherson in his book *Political Theory of Possessive Individualism from Hobbes to Locke*, where he points out that in the capitalist society, individual is considered as the sole proprietor of his skills and owes nothing to society. This leads to possessive thinking. This he traced back to Hobbes in his book *Leviathan*. If the nature of possessive individualism grips family life as it has happened now then such a family can be described as 'having possessive family life'.

References

Brown, Shelby. 1991. *Late Carthaginian Child Sacrifice and Sacrificial Monuments in Their Mediterranean Context*, Sheffield, UK: Sheffield Academic Press.

Hastings, James (ed.). 1955. *Encyclopaedia of Religion and Ethics*, NY: Charles Scribner's Sons.

Hoffer, Peter and N.E.H. Hull. 1981. *Murdering Mothers: Infanticide in England and America 1558–1803*, New York: Oxford University Press.

Hughes, Dennis D. 1991. *Human Sacrifice in Ancient Greece*, London: Routledge.

Milner, Larry S. 2000. *Hardness of Heart/Hardness of Life: The Stain of Human Infanticide*, Lanham/New York/Oxford: University Press of America.

Williamson, Laila. 1978. 'Infanticide: An Anthropological Analysis', in Marvin Kohl (ed.), *Infanticide and the Value of Life*, New York: Prometheus Books.

2

Child Sex Ratios and Gender Discrimination

Challenges for Law and Policy

Mary E. John

When the provisional results of Census 2011 were first announced, newspaper headlines were quite unambiguous in capturing the nation's priorities; first and foremost were the 'positives' – decline in the growth rate of the population, including in the state of Uttar Pradesh (though less than expected for some commentators); a rise in literacy rates; and a rise in the overall sex ratio of the number of women per 1,000 men. The problem was the child sex ratio (CSR, measuring those in the 0–6 year range), which dropped from 927 in 2001 to an all-time low of 914 in 2011. The Secretary to the Home Ministry appeared on the evening news saying that on the matter of the girl child, the government must re-examine its policies.

How should we approach the whole question of sex ratios and the counting of girls? Gender has both become naturalized and a critical instrument in the undisputed aim to control the population, while not allowing the number of females to drop unduly. Even references to gender discrimination are too often subsumed within this larger concern over the role that women play through their fertility patterns in the governance of the population. The inclusion of information on literacy and the 'positive' figure of increased literacy among girls and women are part and parcel of this drive towards ensuring fewer births. At the same time, there are significant relationships between adverse child sex ratios and gender discrimination that need to be addressed. It, therefore, becomes an even greater challenge to look more closely at questions relating to law and policies – those that the government has been promoting specifically to combat the skewed sex ratio – and also other issues, whose effects on the life chances of girls may not be so obvious, but are nonetheless critical. But first, what has been the story so far and what can we learn from Census 2011?

Child Sex Ratios in India Since 1991

In order to begin a discussion of India's child sex ratio patterns, a table (see Table 1) has been prepared that draws from both earlier Census figures and the provisional figures now available. The difference in successive decades has also been included for easy reference. The break-up of the country into the regions of the north–west, north–central, west, east, and south offers a quick overview of broad patterns in the last two decades. (One might keep at the back of our minds not just that this period happens to correspond to the so-called era of neo-liberalism, but also that it spans roughly a generation.) At the national level, the decline of 18 points in the CSR in 2001 has now been followed by a further decline of 13 points. As more families are having fewer children (registered by the reduced fertility rates), there is, therefore, an ongoing gendering in their sex composition. To put it briefly, practices leading to fewer girls in the 0–6 age group have been spreading more thinly during the last decade over a much larger proportion of the country.

The figures from 1991 have been included in order to recall why the Census 2001 made such headlines over a decade ago. This was when the CSR first dropped below that of the overall sex ratio: while the CSR fell from 943 in 1991 to

Table 1

Child Sex Ratios (0–6 years) Census 1991, 2001, 2011, Select States

State	*(Females Per 1,000 Males)*				
	1991	*2001*	*Difference 2001–1991*	*2011*	*Difference 2011–2001*
India	943	927	–18	914	–13
			North–West		
Himachal Pradesh	951	896	–53	906	+10
Punjab	875	798	–77	846	+48
Haryana	879	819	–40	830	+11
Chandigarh	899	845	–46	867	+ 22
Delhi	915	868	–47	866	–2
			North–Central		
Uttar Pradesh	928	916	–12	899	–17
Madhya Pradesh	952	932	–20	912	–20
			West		
Gujarat	928	883	–45	886	+3
Rajasthan	916	909	–7	883	–16
Maharashtra	946	913	–33	883	–30
Goa	964	938	–26	920	–18
			East		
Bihar	959	942	–17	933	–9
Jharkhand	NA	965		943	–22
West Bengal	967	960	–7	950	–10
Nagaland	993	964	–29	944	–20
Odisha	967	953	–14	934	–19
			South		
Andhra Pradesh	975	961	–14	943	–18
Karnataka	960	946	–14	943	–3
Tamil Nadu	948	942	–6	946	+4
Kerala	958	960	+2	959	–1

927 in 2001, that of the overall sex ratio rose from 927 to 933 in the same period (a clear sign that life expectancy among women was increasing significantly). It was in 2001 that several states in north–west India witnessed plunges in their CSRs – with Punjab leading the way by dropping below the 800 mark, while other states, such as Himachal Pradesh, experienced huge declines for the first time. Secondly, 2001 made history (especially at the district level) because of evidence of CSRs falling below the 950 mark (taken as the general norm the world over) in other parts of the country outside the north–west, such as Goa, urban Odisha, and even pockets in the north–east. In the north–west, these patterns were put down to the intensification of practices of sex selection before birth in regions with known prior histories of female infanticide and higher female mortality; elsewhere, a smaller proportion of families were now resorting to similar practices probably for the first time.

Moving on to Census 2011, we find that the state figures point to a clear difference between the north–west and the rest of India. It would appear that there has been a peaking (or plateauing) of the practice of sex selection in states like Gujarat, Haryana, Delhi, and Himachal Pradesh, with small improvements from very low levels in Chandigarh and Punjab (notice that none of the north–western states have fallen further, though they have by no means come back to 1991 levels, which were themselves well below the 950 mark). Punjab's rise from 798 to 846 (48 points) according to 2011 figures makes its CSR similar to that of its neighbours, but only a district-wise analysis would reveal where the real changes are. In Punjab, the severity of the practice has thus eased slightly. In states like Delhi and Gujarat, roughly the same proportion of families are resorting to sex selection as was true a decade ago (since this is a comparison of the number of girl children born and alive between 1996–2001 and 2006–11.) According to district-level data for the state of Haryana, the district of Kurukshetra (which had the worst CSR of 771 in 2001) now has a CSR of 817, similar to the trend for Punjab. However, many more districts (Jhajjar, Mahendergarh, Rewari, Bhiwani, Faridabad, among others) have worse CSRs than in 2001.

Whatever the improvements in north–west India, CSRs are falling in large parts of western, central and eastern India – Maharashtra, Goa, Rajasthan, Madhya Pradesh, Uttar Pradesh, and even Andhra Pradesh has joined the ranks from among the southern states. (Of course, the state of Tamil Nadu is well known for its history of female infanticide and sex selection in districts like Salem and Dharmapuri – so it remains to be seen what a more disaggregated picture of that state would reveal.) In other words, the state-wise figures demonstrate a widening of the circle well beyond the so-called prosperity belt of north–west India, to the poorer states. A recent news report on Uttar Pradesh, for instance, highlights the spread of sex selection to eastern towns and districts where it was hardly known before. Reports from Maharashtra also indicate huge declines in several districts, with the backward district of Beed in the lead recording a massive drop from 894 to 801 between 2001 and 2011. (The only state whose figures are so strange that there is every reason to doubt them is Jammu and Kashmir, where the Census was undertaken after a gap in 1991, 2001, and 2011. According to the provisional figures, the CSR has plummeted from 941 to 859, a drop of 82 points; along with this, Jammu and Kashmir is the only state in the whole country to have registered a positive increase in its fertility during this period. Whatever the form that the ongoing conflict is taking, such figures are hard to make sense of, and require further investigation.)

It is likely that the improvements in the north–west are related to efforts at monitoring the use of sex determination testing, in contrast with its spread elsewhere. Therefore, it would be premature to simply equate an improvement in the sex ratio with less gender discrimination (or vice versa), since the picture is more complex than that. The very fact that the CSRs are falling in such a wide variety of states –

from Goa in the west, which is not associated with high levels of poverty, to poor states like Rajasthan and Madhya Pradesh, and then again with a heterogeneous state like Maharashtra witnessing one of the steepest declines in 2011 of 30 points on average – makes it absolutely necessary to wait for the time when a more contextual micro-level understanding can be undertaken.

An example of such contextual analysis during the previous decade is a study that was conducted by a group of researchers (John et al., 2008) from 2003–05 in five of the lowest CSR districts of north–west India. It became evident that within this broad belt where CSRs had dropped severely, local contexts were nonetheless extremely significant. Thus, for instance, while Fatehgarh Sahib in Punjab demonstrated the presence of families with just one son (especially among Jat Sikhs and urban upper castes) and families in Kangra and Rohtak strived for two children (but very few with only girls), in the districts of Dholpur and Morena, forms of child neglect leading to significant rates of mortality among girls in larger families went hand in hand with the growing practice of sex selection. This essay will be directly concerned with the practice of sex selection as distinct from female infanticide or excess female mortality, because it appears to be the most prominent reason for adverse CSRs. The practice of eliminating the female foetus has been spreading alarmingly, even though efforts have been underway for several decades to combat it.

The Debate Today

In order to get a better perspective on adverse sex ratios, let us recall the decade of the 1980s when practices of amniocentesis for sex selection became the subject of the first campaigns by women's groups and health activists in Maharashtra, Delhi, and Punjab. At that time, this issue garnered little public support; indeed, it was not even clear to most people what the problem was. Today, we might be in the opposite situation, where the sex ratio has become symbolic of gender discrimination as such, and few are interested in anything beyond balancing the numbers. One must underscore the extent of activism and analysis, both in India and abroad, and the range of organizations from local groups, the state, religious organizations, international bodies, and so on, who are closely monitoring these figures.

The results of the Census 2011 have therefore been highly awaited, if from varying perspectives. Some scholars have offered predictions of likely patterns, drawing from the National Family Health Surveys (the most recent being NFHS–3, 2005–06), as well as the Sample Registration at Births (SRBs) made available every year. Significant differences have also been crystallizing. Has there been too great or too little a focus on the law to curb the practice of sex selection? Counter-intuitively, could there be reduced son preference even though the numbers are more skewed than ever before in India's history? Is the problem one of 'mindsets' out of sync with modern values of equality, or, does modernity itself have a lot to do with what is happening? On the one hand, some advocates have been demanding that the main focus must continue to be the effective criminalization of unscrupulous medical practitioners, while others are warning that the very campaigns against sex selection have turned into a problematic, if inadvertent, campaign against abortions per se. While some have predicted heightened practices of 'female genocide', others see signs of a turnaround.

There is something curious about much of this debate and the positions that have been taken. On what basis would we, after all, expect change to happen? Planning the number and sex composition of one's children is surely at the confluence of a range of processes, from stretching limited resources, wanting the 'best' for one's children with the effect of heightening the burden of having them, extreme socio-economic volatility, varying individual morality, the kinds of technologies available, and the nature of gender disparities across classes and groups in contemporary society. A lot has been said about signs of reduced son preference as more and more families say that they want a boy and a girl. But what if this preference actually translates into a willingness to have 'at least one boy, and at most one girl'? Moreover, what kind of structural changes are we witnessing such that expectations of a turnaround could have a genuine basis?

As already mentioned, the Secretary to the Home Ministry went on record to say that in the face of a further decline in the child sex ratio, the state should re-examine its policies. Let us, then, look more closely at what these policies have been. At present, on the legal front, there is the Pre-conception and Pre-natal Diagnostic Techniques Act (PCPNDT), a law explicitly meant to prevent sex selection and most recently revised in 2003. There are also a series of schemes, which have taken the form of conditional cash transfer schemes to families in several states, meant to ease the burden of having a girl child. Whether it is the PCPNDT Act or the schemes, it would appear that these have been far from satisfactory.

Sex Selection and the Law

A brief review of the history of the PCPNDT Act would be instructive in order to gain a better perspective of the difficulties besetting this legislation. It was in the 1980s that women's organizations and health activists discovered that a new technology, amniocentesis testing for foetal abnormalities, was being misused for determining the sex of the foetus, which was followed up with decisions to abort should the foetus be female. The campaigns by the Forum against Sex Determination and Sex Pre-selection (FASDSP) (formed in Bombay in 1985) resulted in an Act by the State of Maharashtra in 1988 to ban sex determination testing in all government establishments and oversee its regulation in the private domain. The first central legislation took the form of the Pre-natal Diagnostic Techniques (Prohibition of Sex Selection) (PNDT) Act of 1994, subsequently revised as the

PC (Pre-conception)–PNDT (Regulation and Prevention of Misuse) Act of 2003. However, legislation by no means had the result that was expected – the practice continued and has been spreading even when it is illegal.

In terms of the legal campaign, it is particularly important to recall that its primary locus has been on the technologies involved in sex determination testing, that is, amniocentesis, specialized pre-selection methods, and ultrasound, and not on the subsequent act of having an abortion (which in any event would not obtain in the rare cases of pre-selection). This point is often missed, given that the campaign is against what is variously termed female foeticide or sex-selective abortions (SSA) and becomes particularly confusing given all the media focus on foetal images or on sensational cases involving the discovery of aborted foetuses. Indeed, till date, there has been no amendment to the Medical Termination of Pregnancy (MTP) Act of 1971 and the conditions under which abortions can be performed. Obviously it is processes whereby the female foetus is eliminated or is not selected that results in 'missing girls' and a skewed sex ratio; but the law as it stands is designed to stem this tide at the first stage of sex determination or pre-selection.[1] As its title suggests, the PNDT Act is an attempt at regulation – naming the techniques, determining where pre-natal diagnostics can be conducted, who can conduct them, procedural aspects of registration, record maintenance, and, finally, provisions for inspection by state-appointed bodies. It is when a breach in such procedures is revealed by the state-monitoring body that a conviction should result, the most significant breach being that the test being conducted is for purposes of sex determination and that the sex of the foetus is disclosed to the pregnant woman. (Punishment includes a jail sentence of up to three years and a fine of ₹ 10,000. For details, see Jaising, 2004.)

In their subsequent examination of the legislative history and context of the PCPNDT Act, Indira Jaising, C. Sathyamala, and Asmita Basu begin by pointing out the first problem with the 1994 legislation – next to nothing was done in terms of its implementation (Jaising et al., 2007). A Public Interest Litigation (PIL) led by Sabu George, CEHAT, and MASUM seeking directions was therefore filed in the Supreme Court in 1998. At this point in time, technological advances available in India included highly expensive and complex possibilities of pre-selection through certain sperm sorting techniques in combination with Assisted Reproductive Technologies (ARTs) to 'choose' the sex of a child at the time of conception through in-vitro fertilization. In flagrant violation of the PNDT Act, even 'home kits' for knowing the sex of a baby have frequently been advertised over the Internet from countries like the US and Canada.

But as Jaising, Sathyamala, and Basu state with great emphasis, it is with the ubiquity of standard ultrasound, prescribed for all pregnancies, that the limits of the law have become most obvious. The law had to be 'prohibitive' in the case of specialized pre-selection practices, but could only be 'regulatory' against the 'misuse' of something like ultrasound, now an integral part of the burgeoning medical business involved in all pregnancy monitoring. Somehow, this regulation had to prevent the communication of the sex of the foetus 'behind closed doors', which, as they point out, could really only be ensured if a legal authority was physically present. In any event, the law had originally been drafted with genetic testing units in mind, not general ultrasound check-ups (ibid.). In other words, the very law meant to curb a specific medical practice has encountered its biggest stumbling block in the fact that what had started out as a particular medical technique to detect foetal abnormalities via specialized genetic centres was now part of the generalized 'normal' practice of ante-natal medical care via ultrasound.

Unlike other forms of neglect or even female infanticide, what makes sex selection unique is that it requires the active intervention by medical personnel and their misuse of medical technology. Medical personnel, moreover, occupy positions of social power and influence, and also legitimacy. While doctors are themselves products of a gender-biased society and may well feel the pressure of vulnerable women who come to them for help in eliminating an unwanted girl, there is no getting away from the fact that 'unlike women, they are not the victims of societal structures. With the power to use medical technology also comes the responsibility to prevent its abuse' (Oommen and Ganatra, 2004: 186). Moreover, they have played their part in the active advertising and spread of the technology of sex selection before it was criminalized. Hence, one of the biggest failures of the PNDT Act has been the immunity of medical practitioners for the most part. While it is commonplace to look for the failure of all our social policies in the realm of implementation (so much so that the language of rights is becoming more and more rhetorical), as far as the PNDT Act is concerned, absolutely nothing was done for several years after the law was first passed in 1994 to put the monitoring bodies in place, leaving no scope for implementation.

It should come as no surprise, then, that extreme measures such as sting operations by news channels with decoy patients have been resorted to in efforts to catch erring doctors. According to Karat and George (2012), there is a strong nexus connecting medical personnel, politicians, and bureaucrats, which has made a mockery of the law:

> Since 1994 when the Pre-conception and Pre-Natal Diagnostic Techniques (Prohibition of Sex Selection) law was enacted, there have been only 93 convictions. Of the 1,036 ongoing cases, only a small per cent, possibly 10 per cent, relate to charges of communication of the sex of the foetus. A majority of the cases are for non-maintenance of records and non-registration of ultrasound machines. Even in cases following widely publicised sting operations of sex determination, no action has been taken against the doctors concerned. For over a decade, the Medical Council of India refused to change its rules to include sex selection as a ground to delicence doctors. In Rajasthan, when the licences of 25 or so doctors were suspended in 2006, following a statewide campaign, the Secretary of the Medical Council, who was held responsible for the

> suspension of the licences by the medical fraternity, was removed and the suspensions rescinded. The DM of Hyderabad was physically assaulted by leading members of the Hyderabad Medical Association because of his efforts to implement the law. (*The Hindu*, 4 February 2012)

It would appear, then, that it is not enough to keep saying that there is nothing wrong with the law (which must certainly be included in any comprehensive policy now under consideration), when its implementation has been either non-existent or so flawed. Moreover, there are other aspects to the law that need more attention. Recall the context in which the PNDT Act was first enacted, namely the introduction of amniocentesis techniques in India meant for the detection of foetal abnormalities. Even though there was some initial discussion among women's organizations about the advisability of demanding a complete ban on any amniocentesis testing, the basic form taken by the law was to make a distinction between 'legitimate' grounds and their 'misuse'. In other words, while checking that certain genetic abnormalities in a foetus are medically and socially acceptable grounds for aborting such a foetus should there be a positive diagnosis, sex determination testing followed by an abortion is a crime. In recent years, disability activists have questioned this taken-for-granted problem of the disabled foetus. Why, they have pertinently asked, should there be such an automatic assumption against bringing a potentially disabled child into the world? What, they go on to suggest, does this tell us about the absence of any effective rights for the disabled and especially of society's responsibilities towards children with disabilities? It is thanks to the efforts of the disability movement that there is at least some awareness of the complexity that surrounds any simple assumptions about 'abnormality'. Politicizing the 'social' bias against girls cannot be advanced without also politicizing the 'naturalised' bias towards disability. By comparing the two – disability and gender – it is therefore apparent that more discussion and advocacy are needed at the interface of both these movements (Ghai, 2008; Ghai and Johri, 2010).

So far this essay has focussed on the major impasses that have been encountered in both creating and implementing the law against sex selection. This does not mean that nothing has or can be achieved through this law. A recent effort has been made to estimate the positive effect of the law by arguing that in its absence, the CSR would have been even more skewed (Nandi and Deolalikar, 2011). The efforts of the Collector at Hyderabad, Arvind Kumar, during his tenure there, in ensuring regular and effective monitoring have been frequently cited as an example of what committed implementation can achieve by way of curbing the practice of sex determination testing. (The city of Hyderabad showed a vastly improved CSR in comparison to neighbouring districts.) Though bureaucrats and politicians have frequently turned to the idea and practice of pregnancy tracking and monitoring as a way forward, it is hugely problematic. This shifts the focus not only from the doctor to the pregnant woman, but also to any decision to undergo an abortion, thus bringing within its ambit abortions that were not preceded by sex determination. Punjab has been using this method of tracking pregnancies by Auxiliary Nurse Midwives (ANMs), especially among women who have had one or two daughters, according to Bijoyalaxmi Nanda (unpublished report). She goes on to say that the improved CSR in Punjab according to Census 2011 has both made the government complacent about any further implementation of the Act and resulted in the withdrawal of donor support to local campaigns, which were quite vibrant a decade ago. The latest effort in the State of Maharashtra has been to introduce a tracking device within ultrasound machines called the 'silent observer', whose purpose is to 'silently' keep an account of all ultrasounds and thereby aid the state in the monitoring of sex determination. Without any prior studies to test its efficacy, it remains to be seen whether this technology will identify erring doctors or display the same problems that accompany the tracking of a pregnancy.

A more positive development in the State of Maharashtra has been the new formation of a coalition of organizations and individuals, the Forum Against Sex Selection (FASS) in the wake of Census 2011. This advocacy group has been particularly vigilant in making clear distinctions between sex determination and sex selective abortion, demanding that the state focus on the former. At the time of writing this article in August 2012, the Maharashtra Government announced that it would treat female foeticide on par with murder, and FASS has been quick to oppose such a move.

Population Policies, Government Schemes, and the Girl Child

This essay began by pointing out the ongoing centrality of governing populations through reducing numbers, and how this compulsion has also affected state action and policies towards combating the adverse child sex ratio. This is glaringly evident when we look at the conditional cash transfer schemes for the girl child being variously promoted by a number of state governments.

At the back of most of these schemes is an aspect of population policy that enjoys widespread consent, namely the two-child norm. Though the National Population Policy (2000) contains no such provisions and though India has been a signatory to the International Conference of Population and Development (ICPD), which entails a commitment to reproductive rights, recent Supreme Court rulings as well as population policies promulgated by several states, including Haryana, Rajasthan, Madhya Pradesh, Chhattisgarh, Odisha, and Andhra Pradesh, seek to penalize and disbar those who have more than two children from accessing various government programmes. First and foremost, such a policy constitutes a violation of human rights, especially, as the National Human Rights Commission noted in 2003, those of 'the marginalized and vulnerable sections of society, including women' (NHRC, 2003: 1). As Mohan Rao has argued, the 'imposition of the two-child norm, and the disincentives proposed (including disbarment to stand for elections right from the level of local government), would mean that the majority of the deprived populations would bear the brunt of the state's withdrawal of ameliorative measures, pitiably inadequate as they are' (Rao, 2008: 301). But, what is less well recognized, in the context of the present focus on adverse CSRs, is that a 'vigorous pursuit of the two-child norm is an invitation to female sex-selective abortion' (ibid.: 303). Indeed, among the more common rationalizations offered by doctors who agree to perform sex determination and sex-selective abortions is precisely their belief that they are helping to bring down population growth. This means that if the state is indeed serious about questioning its policies in the wake of the ongoing decline in the CSR, widespread support for population policies such as the two-child norm, including the introduction of coercive disincentives, must be reviewed if not discontinued.

The paper in this volume by T.V. Sekher provides a detailed desk-based overview of many of the current schemes being promoted in several states. These schemes are all variations of the Girl Child Protection Scheme first launched by the Tamil Nadu government in 1992 in the face of the discovery of female infanticide in certain districts during the 1980s. A sum of ₹ 100 was put into a state fund for each baby girl enrolled in the scheme, followed by further amounts in step with completing various stages of schooling, until finally, at the age of 21, if still unmarried, she would receive a lumpsum of ₹ 20,000. As Rajeswari Sunder Rajan and others have been quick to point out, however, this scheme was further saddled with various eligibility criteria – no sons, indeed, subsequent sterilization of the mother to ensure no further births, and BPL income levels for a family that wished to enrol (Sunder Rajan, 2003). While the amounts of money have increased in the interim, if anything, the conditionalities and eligibility criteria for the various schemes on offer today, as discussed by Sekher, have multiplied. Moreover, the scrambling of population control with protecting the girl child is particularly problematic. Poverty has also been turned into an eligibility criterion when it is well known that planning the gender of one's children is at its most acute among the non-poor; that is, among those striving for upward mobility with limited resources. Many have critiqued such schemes for effectively providing a lumpsum as dowry to a family – and in north–west India, the 'ladli' scheme is locally called 'dahej' (dowry) scheme. It is to be hoped therefore that these schemes will be subjected to much needed review.

Dowry and Beyond

In the early years of sex determination testing, when medical practitioners openly advertised their services, a common slogan found on roadsides and in suburban trains was 'spend ₹ 500 now and save ₹ 50,000 later'. This invitation to rationalize supply and demand through a simple financial calculation – pay doctors a fraction for a girl's elimination before birth and be spared her dowry – is surely crass. Yet, it clearly touched and continues to touch a nerve – indeed, the battle against dowry is one of the oldest struggles of the women's movement. According to historians like Veena Talwar Oldenburg, the rise in dowry (over bride price) during the 19th century among several castes in colonial Punjab, which was a consequence of changes in British revenue policy, resulted in a parallel spurt in female infanticide. She sees an ongoing parallel today with dowry deaths and sex selection (Oldenburg, 2002). Even Brinda Karat and Sabu George, in their recent discussion on the need for a comprehensive policy to target the declining sex ratio, state at the outset that the government must act against the menace of dowry being driven by the consumerist policies of the country. As they put it: 'Like a black shadow in the wake of dowry demands, is the spread of sex selection' (Karat and George, 2012). It is perhaps not accidental, then, that the National Commission for Women at the time of writing is engaged in reviewing the Dowry Prohibition Act, another one of our laws that has been supremely lacking in the capacity for implementation.

There are a number of important issues here that we must look at, as we turn now to the 'demand' side with more and more families seeking recourse to sex selection. Dowry represents the payments in cash and kind that have come to accompany the marriage of a daughter, and there is considerable evidence that it has been spreading and increasing over time. (The obverse, which is often not openly mentioned, is that having a son also means expectations of receiving a hefty dowry at the time of his marriage.) The first point being made here, given that this essay is appearing in a volume on children, is the somewhat transient place that a child occupies in the course of a given life. When parents are attempting to actually plan the number and sex composition of their children, it is not childhood that is on their horizon. They are planning to have or not have a daughter or a son who will have to be brought up into adulthood, 'settled', and whose future relationship will be shaped by the inter-generational transfer of resources. This is also why the image of the 'girl child' who must be 'saved' (as in Beti Bachao campaigns) may not actually name the problem that is driving the changing nature of son preference and daughter aversion today. Growing daughter aversion is about wishing to be spared the burden of bringing up a girl into an adult woman, with all the attendant costs involved.

Secondly, while dowry no doubt has its place, the new levels reached by adverse CSRs require a correspondingly multidimensional level of analysis and cannot simply rest content with dowry as a one-size-fits-all phenomenon symbolizing gender discrimination. No one factor – be it available technologies on the supply side or heightened demands for dowry – can stand in for the combination of factors that are at work. Technologies may well be closing the gap between demand and supply; but are not, for all that, an independently causal factor, since the southern states, with the longest histories of medicalization of pregnancies, have not become leaders in sex selection. There is no question that fertility declines have set in and are spreading across the country, aided by population policies as well as, when it comes to the non-poor, by more voluntary 'choices' to have fewer children. Contemporary India is witnessing a highly gendered version of this choice – in north–west India, according to the findings of the study already cited earlier (John et al., 2008), this veers from one to three children. It is worth underscoring that this marks an unprecedented shift in son preference as well and that extra sons are no longer wanted either. Family planning now means planning for one or two sons and allowing for the birth of at most one daughter. It would surely be worth exploring whether this dynamic has now moved beyond north–west India into the swathe of the country that has seen a downward spiral over the last decade.

What kind of broader analyses are therefore required? While much has been said about the north–west being the most prosperous region of the country, this prosperity, especially post-green revolution, requires a much more nuanced analysis. A huge disenchantment with agriculture characterizes this region, supplemented by highly volatile socio-economic forms of development. At the same time, modern changes are palpable – such as increase in educational attainments, and rise in the ages of marriage. 'These unintended consequences of contemporary social processes, when combined with parental fears of the unattached sexuality of adult daughters in a context of a highly competitive and differentiated marriage market, are compounding the sense of burden represented by the birth of a daughter. She now requires many more years at home with higher investments in nutrition, health and education... Sons, on the other hand, embody a range of ritual and economic roles. If the current climate of economic volatility and masculine anomie makes them often fall short of expectations, nonetheless at least one is essential for the future of the family. It is this conjuncture that is producing the falling child sex ratio' (ibid.: 86).

There has been far too much focus on the need to restore the 'balance' to the skewed numbers and on quick-fix solutions. What is forgotten is that, in a growing population like ours with its hypergamous marriage market, male privilege has benefited over the course of the last century from an excess of marriageable women in any given cohort. In other words, there has been an invisible structural imbalance at work in most parts of the country outside the north–west, but which was never considered to be a problem to be 'corrected'. (The peculiar case of Kerala with its positive sex ratio but highly discriminatory practices against women is a case in point.) Furthermore, in most of the discussion on fertility and sex ratios, little attention is given to what is arguably the most critical indicator of the status of gender in our country. According to Indrani Mazumdar and N. Neetha, the 64th Round of the National Sample Survey (2007–08) has the stunning revelation that after twenty years of unprecedented economic growth, the total proportion of women in any kind of paid work is no more than 15 per cent. Another way of putting this would be to say that 85 per cent of all women are destined to find their future through structural forms of dependency, namely marriage. This does not even begin to discuss the nature of the work that constitutes the 15 per cent (Mazumdar and Neetha, 2011).

This means that beyond the practice of dowry, a larger canvas is discernable, which begins with the social, educational, and sexual burdens experienced in bringing up a daughter. This does not simply conclude with the compulsory nature of marriage that takes her away, since it may not represent the end of parental responsibilities for her. While it is commonplace to think of these as aspects of contemporary culture with longer traditional roots in India's history, we cannot neglect to notice how well this fits in with the pattern of economic growth that we have been witnessing, one that is generating a revolution in modes of consumption, but precious few opportunities of economic security for women in the new labour market.

If indeed the government is serious about reconsidering its policies in the wake of the declining CSR, then it must recognize the range of policies that are shaping the futures of today's girls and boys. Surely, the government has to show greater political will in exposing the nexus between medical practitioners and the political machinery, if the law against sex selection is to have any chance of making sex selection a crime. But, unless both government and society acknowledge how 'choices' for having a girl are at the confluence of policies relating to access to health, education, sexual safety, and economic viability, it is unlikely that we will see any lasting impact on the sex ratio, much less curtail its further spread.

Note

1. Nivedita Menon challenged the campaign against sex selection by arguing that the very effort to obtain justice from the law is doomed to be a failure. It is simply philosophically incoherent to argue in favour of abortion 'in terms of the right of women to control their bodies and at the same time, demanding that women be restricted by law from choosing specifically to abort female fetuses' (Menon, 2004: 72). Abortion in other parts of the world already encountered problems when deploying the language of rights because of the ways in which foetal rights were then placed in opposition to those of the mother. In our context, Menon asks how the law can be 'selective'; that is to say, distinguish between a general right to abortion, on the one hand, and the specific abrogation of that right in the case of sex selection. However, as I have indicated, the law itself is not focussed on abortion per se, but rather on the prior process of sex determination.

References

Ghai, Anita. 2008. 'A Disabled Feminism?', in Mary E. John (ed.), *Women's Studies in India*, New Delhi: Penguin.

Ghai, Anita and Rachna Johri. 2010. (Article name missing?), in Renu Adlakkha (ed.), *Indian Journal of Gender Studies, Special Issue on Disability and Gender.*

Jaising, Indira, C. Sathyamala and Asmita Basu. 2007. *From the Abnormal to the Normal: Preventing Sex Selective Abortions Through the Law*, New Delhi: Lawyers Collective.

Jaising, Indira (ed.). 2004. *Pre-conception and Pre-natal Diagnostic Techniques Act: A Users Guide to the Law*, New Delhi: Universal Law Publishing Co.

John, Mary E., Ravinder Kaur, Rajni Palriwala, Saraswati Raju and Alpana Sagar. 2008. *Planning Families, Planning Gender: The Adverse Child Sex Ratio in Selected Districts of Punjab, Haryana, Himachal Pradesh, Rajasthan and Madhya Pradesh*, Bangalore: Books for Change.

Karat, Brinda and Sabu George. 2012. 'Don't Trash This Law: The Problem Lies in Implementation', *The Hindu*, 4 February.

Mazumdar, Indrani and N. Neetha. 2011. 'Gender Dimensions: Employment Trends in India, 1993–94 to 2009–10', *Economic and Political Weekly*, Vol. 46, No. 43.

Menon, Nivedita. 2004. *Recovering Subversion: Feminist Politics Beyond the Law*, Urbana, IL: University of Illinois Press.

Nanda, Bijoyalaxmi. 2013. 'Does the Girl-child Count? Census and Other Stories', *Mainstream*, Vol. LI, No. 15, pp. 1-5.

Nandi, Arindam and Anil B. Deolalikar. 2011. 'Does a Legal Ban on Sex Selective Abortions Improve Child Sex Ratios? Evidence from a Policy Change in India', *Journal of Development Economics*, April.

National Human Rights Commission. 2003. *Declaration: National Colloquium on Population Policies*, New Delhi.

Oldenburg, Veena Talwar, 2002. *Dowry Murder: The Imperial Origins of a Cultural Crime*, Delhi: Oxford University Press.

Oommen, Nandini and Bela R. Ganatra. 2004. 'Sex Selection: The Systematic Elimination of Girls', *Reproductive Health Matters*, Vol. 10, No. 19.

Rao, Mohan. 2008. 'Population Policy and the Two Child Norm', in Mary E. John (ed.), *Women's Studies in India*, New Delhi: Penguin.

Sunder Rajan, Rajeswari. 2003. 'Children of the State? Unwanted Girls in Tamil Nadu', in *The Scandal of the State: Women, Law and Citizenship in Postcolonial India*, New Delhi: Permanent Black.

3

Eliminating Daughters

An Unfortunate Reality of West and North–West India

Anjali Radkar

Indian society is mostly patriarchal, patrilineal and patrilocal and that is one of the most probable reasons for the preference for sons over daughters. Son preference in India is universal and ancient. It actually is an indicator of social development. It portrays the social inequality and lower status of women in the society. The preference is influenced by various socio-economic and cultural factors. It is mainly the reflection of the wide gap in the differentials of roles of girls and boys. Looking at cost benefits, sons are always valued better than daughters. In this context, they are considered as assets and daughters as liability. Actually, having a son is looked upon as a package for successful, smooth life rather than a single isolated cause. Along with the lineage and old-age support, psychological satisfaction of having a son and inner need to feel complete are the causes of the desire for sons.

Son preference is observed in all cross-sections of the society, though the extent varies. During earlier period, the family size was large and in a large family, balance of number of sons and daughters was naturally maintained. As family size started coming down, son preference became visible. In a small family of two or one, it became difficult to get the desired sex composition of children. Those who did not get a son started making use of technology, pre-natal diagnostic techniques to predetermine the sex of the foetus – the technology that basically came into practice to detect the congenital malformations or genetic abnormalities in the foetus. Sex determination followed by abortion of the female foetus or in other words sex-selective abortions have a direct impact on the number of girls born and thus on the overall number of women in the society. These practices on a large scale manifested as a distorted proportion of males and females in the population.

Sex Ratio

Sex ratio, a proxy indicator of son preference, is defined as the number of females per 1,000 males. Sex ratio was less in India since census started and it is declining consistently. Generally men outnumber women and sex ratio is low in India. Biologically women are the stronger sex. So in

Chart 1

Sex Ratio and Child Sex Ratio, India

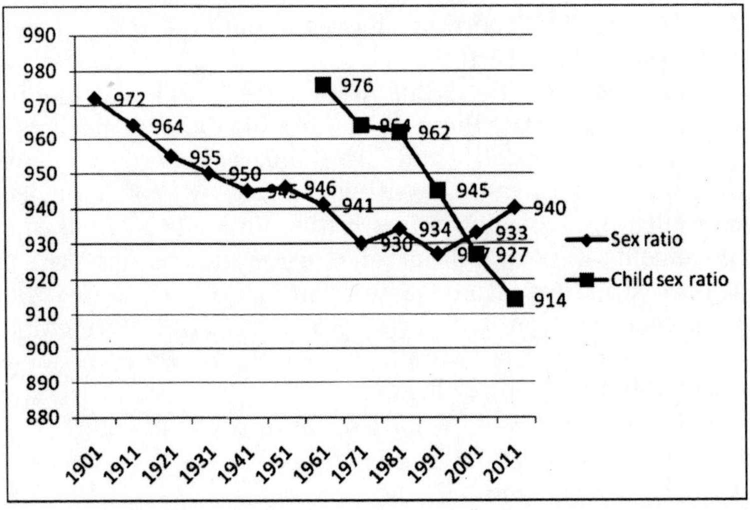

societies where women and men are treated equally, women outlive men so that there would be more women than men in the adult population.

The sex ratio situation in India in this century is presented in Chart 1. It indicates the deficit of females in Indian population for the past 110 years. Sex ratio has always been unfavourable for females and has a declining trend. When the British conducted the first-ever census in 1872, they were shocked to see the deficit of females in the population – a situation contrary to their country. During 1961–1971, the country experienced the sharpest decline of 11 points from 941 to 930. Then onwards, sex ratio has been fluctuating around 930. During 2001–2011, an increase from 933 to 940 is a welcome improvement.

Sex ratio of Indian population has always been the topic of interest to demographers, social scientists, women's groups, researchers, planners and policy-makers. Why such uneven sex composition, compared to developed countries in the world? Several reasons come out to explain the consistently low levels of sex ratio and its further decline, like

- Neglect of the girl child resulting in higher mortality at younger ages.
- High maternal mortality.
- Sex-selective abortions, female infanticide and changes in sex ratio at birth.

From data quality point of view, sex is an easily identifiable characteristic, therefore getting the data on the sex is easy. Fertility, mortality and migration are three components of population change. Fertility is associated with births, mortality is associated with deaths, and migration is the movement of people from one region to another. Thus, sex-age structure of any population also is determined by past trends of fertility, mortality and migration. Stretching this concept further, overall sex ratio is the result of joint effect of following three factors:

1. The sex ratio of new-born babies or sex ratio at birth
2. The sex ratio of deceased persons
3. The sex ratio of migrants

Biologically, sex ratio at birth is 943–952 girls per 1,000 boys. This means for any birth cohort, there are about 950 girls for 1,000 boys. Sex ratio at birth is a biological phenomenon so does not differ from population to population and it would not alter in a short period of time unless there is a human intervention. Sex ratio at birth thus is always favourable to males considering the fact that males are biologically weaker than females. Initial excess of males over females naturally balances their proportion in the population over a long period.

Sex ratio of deceased persons is nearly balanced. Earlier high mortality of women was a major determinant for lesser women in the population, but during the recent times health of women has improved. It is evident from the increased life expectancy of females than males. According to latest projections for 2011–2015, expectation of life at birth for males would be 67.3 years and for females 69.6 years. In the last decade, life expectancy of males and females maintained the difference of over 2 years. It shows that sex differentials in mortality or the sex ratio of deceased persons has a limited impact on the overall sex ratio.

As regards migration, it is either internal or international. Considering the size of Indian population, share of international migration is negligible so the sex ratio of international migrants would not make a dent on sex ratio of India. When we discuss the sex ratio at a national level, the effect of migration does not really play any role.

Child Sex Ratio

Child sex ratio is the sex ratio of children in the age group 0–6 years. It gives the recent picture of the existing situation. Chart 1 indicates that child sex ratio has gone down from 976 in 1961 to 964 in 1971 to 962 in 1981 to 945 in 1991 to 927 in 2001 and further 914 in 2011. It was much higher initially than the overall sex ratio. It declined below sex ratio after 2001. It has decreased at a much faster pace than the overall sex ratio after 1981. The decreasing child sex ratio has a cascading effect on a population over a period of time, leading to diminishing sex ratio in the country. This imbalance that has set in at this early age-group is difficult to be removed and would remain to disturb the population for a long time to come. Demographically, the child sex ratio of 914 does not appear to predict well for the future of the country.

Overall sex ratio has been declining steadily over more than 110 years and is a cause of concern; but the sharp decline in child sex ratio from 962 in 1981 to 914 in 2011 is a shocking reflection of our society. Information about child sex ratio explains the recent conditions existing in the society. It can also be taken as proxy to sex ratio at birth. These figures tell more about the current and therefore future imbalance of males and females. Overall child sex ratio of India depends on the sex ratio of states and Union Territories, which shows large differentials. This diversity is phenomenal. Child sex ratio figures for major states for the period 1961 to 2011 are presented in Table 1.

Table 1

Child Sex Ratio, India and Major States, 1961–2011

States	*1961*	*1971*	*1981*	*1991*	*2001*	*2011*
India	976	964	962	945	927	914
Punjab	894	899	908	875	793	846
Haryana	910	898	902	879	820	830
Delhi	923	909	926	915	865	866
Rajasthan	951	933	954	916	909	883
Gujarat	955	946	947	928	878	886
Maharashtra	978	978	956	946	917	883
Bihar	988	964	981	953	938	933
Madhya Pradesh	982	976	978	941	929	912
Uttar Pradesh	946	923	935	927	916	899
Odisha	1,035	1,168	995	967	950	934
West Bengal	1,008	1,010	981	967	963	950
Andhra Pradesh	1,002	990	992	975	964	943
Karnataka	987	978	975	960	949	943
Kerala	972	976	970	958	963	959
Tamil Nadu	985	974	967	948	939	946

Though child sex ratio for India in 2011 was 914, many states in the country registered it as 900. Pre-natal sex selection is considered to be the leading cause for the missing girls and an imbalanced child sex ratio. While child sex ratio is principally determined by the sex ratio at birth, it is also influenced by a number of other factors such as under-registration of girls, differential infant and child mortality, and age misreporting. Therefore, the imbalance in child sex ratio cannot be entirely attributed to the practice of pre-natal sex selection (UNFPA, 2010), though its large share is today's unfortunate reality.

Child sex ratio is decreasing and it is decreasing at a much faster rate especially after 1981. For all the states, there is a big jump down after 1981. During 1981–1991, Punjab, Haryana, Rajasthan, Bihar, Madhya Pradesh and Odisha showed a large decline. In the next decade between 1991 and 2001, along with Punjab and Haryana three other states, namely Delhi, Gujarat and Maharashtra showed a much larger difference. That is the reason why states in the North–West and West came in forefront of the debate about missing girls. Southern states more or less kept the balance though some variations were observed there as well.

Sex Ratio at Birth

Sex ratio at birth is the number of girls born for every 1,000 boys born. It is a more accurate and refined indicator of the extent of pre-natal sex selection. The comparison of observed sex ratio at birth with the biological sex ratio at birth gives an idea of girls missing at birth. The imbalance in the number of males and females begins in the beginning. It is a well established law of nature that males exceed females at the time of birth. It is believed that generally 943–952 female births take place for every 1,000 male births, which in effect means that there is a deficiency of about 50 females per 1,000 males in every birth cohort. Many demographers believe that it is an unalterable constant. But what is happening around tells a different story, as the deficit is much more than 50. The data on sex ratio at birth for past many years obtained from Sample Registration System (SRS) is indicative of the larger than usual shortfall in female births compared to male births. For the period of 1980–1998, average sex ratio at birth was around 900. Thus, for the recent period, there is some primary evidence that sex ratio at birth for the country as a whole is possibly lower than the generally accepted 943–952.

Table 2

Sex Ratio at Birth, 1998–2008

	2006–2008	*2005–2007*	*2004–2006*	*2003–2005*	*2001–2003*	*2000–2002*	*1999–2001*	*1998–2000*
India	904	901	892	880	883	892	894	898
Andhra Pradesh	917	915	917	917	932	945	934	960
Assam	933	939	920	907	904	945	962	984
Bihar	914	909	881	965	861	870	873	896
Chhattisgarh	975	969	961	947				
Delhi	877	871	847	831				
Gujarat	898	891	865	844	862	844	837	851
Haryana	847	843	837	829	807	804	803	797
Himachal Pradesh	938	931	872	858	803	826	858	902
J&K	862	854	838	824				
Jharkhand	922	927	888	872				
Karnataka	935	926	917	915	943	952	935	942
Kerala	964	958	922	912	892	911	927	930
M. Pradesh	919	913	913	911	922	920	915	907
Maharashtra	884	871	879	872	887	899	915	913
Odisha	937	933	934	932	934	944	920	928
Punjab	836	837	808	801	776	775	775	792
Rajasthan	870	865	855	839	855	890	885	877
Tamil Nadu	936	944	955	943	953	926	926	931
Uttar Pradesh	877	881	874	862	853	864	870	868
West Bengal	941	936	931	926	937	949	956	952

Source: Sample Registration System.

Data on sex ratio at birth is periodically collected at the national level by the Civil Registration System and the Sample Registration System (SRS). These reports are published annually by the Office of the Registrar General of India. The Civil Registration System data is not reliable due to gross under-registration of births in some states. Hence, SRS estimates are the most frequently used and quoted source of sex ratio at birth data. These estimates provide results at state and national level, but not for the district level. Since sampling errors for annual estimates could be large, the SRS gives three-year moving averages of the sex ratio at birth rather than a single year.

As far as the sex ratio at birth is concerned, there is a lot of variation among the states. Very few states are closer to normal range, i.e. 943–952. Kerala has it more – the recent estimate is 964. The data also shows a slightly upward trend after 2003–2005 which is reflected in the child sex ratio of 2011, especially in states like Punjab, Haryana, Delhi, Himachal Pradesh and Gujarat, where the child sex ratio was worst affected.

Sex ratio at birth in India for the period 2006–2008 was 904, which actually is less. However, an important fact is that it is showing an upward trend. The states with low child sex ratio in 2001 show an improvement in sex ratio at birth and that is reflected in child sex ratio of 2011. Still, it is estimated that the practice of pre-natal sex selection has resulted in approximately 0.6 million girls being missed annually in India during the period 2001–2007. This is roughly 1,600 girls a day (UNFPA, 2010).

Based on the sex ratio at birth, the share of the missing girls is highest for Punjab (16.2%), followed by Haryana (12.9%) and Jammu and Kashmir (10.5%).

Then are the states like Delhi, Rajasthan, Gujarat, Uttar Pradesh, Himachal Pradesh, Bihar and Maharashtra having a share between 8.9 per cent and 5.9 per cent. These percentages are translated into huge numbers. Missing girls at such an extent is very demeaning for any country.

Table 3

Estimates of the Missing Girls in India

States	*Estimated number of female births that did not occur each year due to pre-natal sex selection*	*Per cent missing female births (out of total female births)*
Punjab	35,833	16.2
Haryana	33,588	12.9
Jammu and Kashmir	9,987	10.5
Delhi	11,883	8.9
Rajasthan	71,931	8.7
Gujarat	47,503	7.9
Uttar Pradesh	1,95,899	7.6
Himachal Pradesh	4,468	7.6
Bihar	76,160	6.0
Maharashtra	55,053	5.9
Jharkhand	12,718	3.4
Madhya Pradesh	17,261	1.9
Kerala	3,697	1.5
Andhra Pradesh	8,621	1.1
Assam	3,232	1.1
Karnataka	1,942	0.3
India	6,01,468	4.8

North–West and West

Trends in child sex ratio as well as sex ratio at birth show that the states from North–West and West are the culprits. They are responsible for the lesser number of females in the population. All these are economically developed states. Probably this prosperity leads to sex-selective abortions, where they have resources and access to these techniques. Expression of son preference in this manner is severe. A survey in Delhi reported that highly educated women have resorted to repeated abortions to ensure that they will give birth only to a son. It endorses that education and economic progress do not change the mindset (UNFPA, 2003). Education and income are related and are determinants of low fertility. As discussed before, son preference becomes more visible when family size goes down, and is reflected in lower child sex ratio. Along with education, if status of women is high, child sex ratio would not be as low. Kerala is one such state in India.

The drop in child sex ratio after 1981 is indicative of sex-selective abortions of female foetus. That was the period when use of pre-natal diagnostic techniques such as ultrasound, for the purpose of detecting genetic abnormalities or other sex-linked disorders of the foetus, came into practice. Initially when pre-natal sex selection came, it was thought as a problem of metros, limited only to better-off who could afford the technology. No one expected that within two decades, sex-detection techniques would become so widespread and affordable that they would be available all over the country with devastating consequences on child sex ratio.

The study on registration of clinics having ultrasound machines conducted in Maharashtra indicated that where the availability of the technology is more, child sex ratio is less (Nagarajan and Mulay, 2008). The story cannot be different for other states.

It has become evident now that states from North–Western part followed by Western part are much more responsible for the decline of sex ratio and child sex ratio at the national level. It is necessary to look at those states more critically on what was the situation historically and how it is now. These states were discriminating the most. All of these are rich and developed states. They have health facilities and health systems delivery better than most of the other Northern part of India.

Sex ratio figures for North–Western states are consistently on the lower side historically. For the past 110 years, sex ratio of Punjab, Haryana, Delhi and Jammu and Kashmir has not crossed the 900-mark even once. On the contrary, sex ratio of

Himachal Pradesh is slightly higher than these states and it has improved considerably in the past 50 years. Substantial improvement in sex ratio and child sex ratio figures for Punjab, Haryana and Delhi in 2011 is an achievement.

Table 4

Sex Ratio of North–Western and Western States, 1901–2011

Year	*North–Western States*				*Western States*			
	Punjab	*Haryana*	*Delhi*	*Himachal Pradesh*	*J&K*	*Rajasthan*	*Gujarat*	*Maharashtra*
1901	832	867	862	884	882	905	954	978
1911	780	835	793	889	876	908	946	966
1921	799	844	733	890	870	896	944	950
1931	815	844	722	897	865	907	945	947
1941	836	869	715	890	869	906	941	949
1951	844	871	768	912	873	921	952	941
1961	854	868	785	938	878	908	940	936
1971	865	867	801	958	878	911	934	930
1981	879	870	808	973	892	919	942	937
1991	882	865	827	976	896	910	934	934
2001	874	864	821	970	900	922	921	922
2011	893	877	866	974	883	926	918	925

Western states have a different story. Their sex ratio figures are much higher than that of North–Western states. Rajasthan is improving consistently over the period though the figures are on the lower side of the scale. On the contrary, Gujarat and Maharashtra started better but are getting worse. Both these states show a consistent decline. In 2011, Maharashtra has slightly gone up. Now referring to Table 2, it is becoming clear that Maharashtra's situation is actually worse because child sex ratio there has gone down to 883 from 917. It is an all-time low figure. On the contrary, Gujarat child sex ratio has slightly gone up though it is still at 886. Child sex ratio for Rajasthan also has gone down to 883 from 909. Therefore, though there is a slight increase in overall sex ratio of the states, child sex ratio is decreasing. This is an alarming situation.

To Conclude

Historically, North–West part of India has been eliminating daughters and sex ratio is very low there. Recent estimates of sex ratio and child sex ratio there show an upward trend and it is a sigh of relief. Still the figures need to go up considerably. In 2011, West has come on the forefront. States of Rajasthan, Gujarat and Maharashtra were just behind North–West and are grabbing attention in terms of low child sex ratio. Decline in Maharashtra and Rajasthan is alarming whereas Gujarat has improved but still the figures are on the lower side. Actually, the entire West and also North–West need action to improve their figures and in turn India figures.

According to Nobel laureate Amartya Sen, India with its huge population has to account for millions of 'missing women'. These are mainly the girls not born. Overall sex ratio has been declining and the major contributing factor is the decline in child sex ratio. This decline in child sex ratio is mostly the result of the preference for son, two-child norm – either the state policy or because of economic compulsions – and sex determination techniques. Thus, to improve the situation, it is necessary to enhance the status of women so that preference for sons would go down and in turn sex-selective abortions would reduce. Declining sex ratio would have far-reaching social consequences. As a major consequence, women would become the targets of violence. Polyandry would become a modern-day reality. Some women's groups believe that the declining number of females in the society would enhance the value of women in terms of their status. But no evidence of this sort is available till date.

It is clear now that misuse of pre-natal diagnostic techniques for sex determination, sex-selective abortions and infanticide are rapidly declining child sex ratio. Unless urgent action is taken across all sectors to reverse this trend, to eliminate gender discrimination and restore balance of girls and boys in the population, its social repercussions for future generations would be devastating. Then, could we any more call ourselves 'cultured'?

References

Census of India. 2011. Population Tables, Census of India, Office of Registrar General, India, Ministry of Home Affairs, Government of India, New Delhi.

Kulkarni, P.M. 2007. 'Estimation of Missing Girls at Birth and Juvenile Ages in India', United Nations Population Fund, India.

Nagarajan, R. and S. Mulay. 2008. 'Ultrasound Sonography Centres and Child Sex Ratio Across Maharashtra: A District Level Analysis', *Artha Vijnana*, Vol. 50, No. 4, December, pp. 433–48.

Sample Registration System. 2008. Sample Registration System Statistical Report 2007, Office of Registrar General, India, Ministry of Home Affairs, Government of India, New Delhi.

UNFPA. 2003. 'Missing: Mapping the Adverse Child Sex Ratio in India', Office of Registrar General and Census Commissioner, India, Ministry of Health and Family Welfare, New Delhi.

——. 2010. 'Trends in Sex Ratio at Birth and Estimates of Girls Missing at Birth', United Nations Population Fund, India.

4

Eliminating Daughters and Selecting Sons

Planning Families

Neerja Ahlawat

The continuing trend of skewed sex ratio, particularly the child sex ratio (CSR), has perplexed social scientists and policy planners. Earlier, it was attributed to higher mortality levels among females than males. However, the juvenile sex ratio shows massive declines in each census. The nationwide overall sex ratio (the number of females per thousand males) in 2011 Census has shown an improvement of seven points, i.e. from 933 in 2001 Census to 940 in 2011 Census. This is the highest sex ratio so far at the national level since 1971 Census. What is perplexing the minds of social scientists, demographers and policy planners is the further decline in child sex ratio from 927 in 2001 Census to 914 in 2011 Census. It shows that intolerance towards the girl child continues despite the implementation of PCPNDT.

The worst gender ratios, indicating gross gender imbalance, are found in South and East Asian countries such as India and China. The pre-birth sex selection of the foetus by ultrasound scanning, amniocentesis, and in-vitro fertilization has aggravated this situation. Female foetuses are selectively aborted after pre-natal sex determination, thus avoiding the birth of girls. As a result of selective abortion, around 35 to 40 million girls are missing from the Indian population. Amartya Sen (1990) drew the attention of the nation towards the 'missing women phenomena' that with its present population of 120 crore people, we have to make an account of some 25 million 'missing women'. If western standards were applied, India too should have had about 105 women for every 100 men today. Thus, there should have been 512 million women in India. Female foeticide is an extreme manifestation of poor status of women, who are socially constructed as an inferior and less valuable sex and often projected as a burden on the family. The risk faced by the girl child appears to be more acute in areas which have strongly benefited from the ongoing process of rapid economic change, and consequent considerable changes in the social fabric of society. It has been estimated that approximately 0.5 million girls have been denied being born during the past two decades. Clearly, there is a stronger bias against girl children, particularly among the rich and the educated Indians.

The issue of unfavourable sex ratio in India is not a recent one; it gained the attention of colonial rulers during British time as well. The historical evidences of female infanticide and infant mortality in North and North–West India have very well been recorded (Premi, 2001; Agnihotri, 2000; Mitra, 2001; Vishwanath, 2004). The killing of girl babies has a long history in North–West India and remains quite common in particular areas and communities (Premi and Raju, 1996). In post-Independence India, the phenomenon was brought forward in the late '60s and '70s by demographers who witnessed a declining trend from the turn of 20th century onwards. The deficit of daughters, which was not evident in 1981, except in historically masculine states such as Punjab and Haryana, became quite evident by 2001 in states like Himachal Pradesh, Gujarat, Rajasthan, Madhya Pradesh and Maharashtra. It was in these states that private sex determination clinics were first established and the practice of selective abortion became popular from the late

1970s. Eminent demographer Asish Bose (2001) coined an interesting term DEMARU (daughter elimination and male craze for ultrasound) and categorically remarked about Haryana as DEMARU or daughter *maru* state.

Many studies show how cultural practices have always undervalued daughters or women in Indian society (Miller, 1981; Dasgupta, 1987; Minturn, 1993; Sudha and Rajan, 1999). In Tamil Nadu, the districts of Madurai and Dharampuri have exceptionally few girls and have been in the news for the alleged murder of baby girls. Tanumanji, a village in Barmer, Rajasthan, recorded 245 girls per thousand boys (2001 Census). If we look at data on life expectancy at birth and crude death rate by sex, it is quite clear that in the last few years, life expectancy for females has improved considerably and female death rates have also come down. This has further resulted in an improvement in overall sex ratio in the country and in majority of states, which is evident from the 2011 Census data.

Child Sex Ratio (0–6 years)

While the overall sex ratio presents somewhat encouraging trends across the country, the same is not true in the case of the girl child in the age group 0–6 years. There is a sharp decline in child sex ratio from 976 in 1961 Census to 914 in 2011 Census. Table 1 shows a declining trend in the child sex ratio (0–6 years).

Table 1

Overall Sex Ratio and Child Sex Ratio from 1961–2011 Census

Year	*Overall Sex Ratio*	*Child Sex Ratio (0–6)*
1961	941	976
1971	930	964
1981	934	962
1991	927	945
2001	933	927
2011	940	914

Source: Census 2001 and 2011.

Inter-State Variations in Child Sex Ratio

There are sharp inter-state variations in CSR. The lowest child sex ratio (0–6 years) among the states has been observed in the states of Haryana (830), Punjab (846) and Jammu and Kashmir (859), while among the UTs, Delhi (866), Chandigarh (867) and Lakshadweep (908) occupy the bottom position.

As regards the rising trend in CSR in Census 2011, child sex ratio (0–6 years) has registered an increasing trend only in six states and two UTs. What gives some cause for cheer is the fact that the states where the child sex ratio had dropped alarmingly in Census 2001 have now shown a slight improvement. This increase is substantial in Punjab (789 to 846 – 57 points), Haryana (819 to 830 – 11 points), Himachal Pradesh (896 to 906 – 10 points), Chandigarh (845 to 867 – 22 points), Gujarat (883 to 886 – 3 points) and Tamil Nadu (942 to 946 – 4 points). In addition, Mizoram (964 to 971 – 7 points) and Andaman and Nicobar Islands (957 to 966 – 9 points) have also shown an increasing trend in the child sex ratio during 2001–2011.

At the same time, the situation in other states/UTs has been disconcerting. The child sex ratio (0–6 years) has declined in 27 states and Union Territories. Sharp fall in the range of 22 to 82 points has been reported in child sex ratios in Jammu and Kashmir (82), Dadra and Nagar Haveli, Lakshadweep, Maharashtra, Rajasthan, Manipur, Uttarakhand, Jharkhand, Madhya Pradesh, and Nagaland during 2001–2011. It is to be noticed that even North–Eastern states like Sikkim and Arunachal Pradesh have shown a declining trend.

Bottom 10 Districts with Lowest Child Sex Ratio

Censuses 2001 and 2011 list the bottom 10 districts with lowest child sex ratios. Some of the districts that had the lowest child sex ratio in 2001 Census gained in 2011 Census whereas some new districts such as Samba in Jammu and Kashmir and Beed in Maharashtra registered sharp declines in child sex ratio and were included in the list of bottom 10 districts.

Table 2

Bottom 10 Districts According to Child Sex Ratio (0–6 age group)

Census 2001			*Census 2011*		
District	*State*	*CSR*	*District*	*State*	*CSR*
Fatehgarh Sahib	Punjab	766	Jhajjar	Haryana	774
Patiala	Punjab	777	Mahendergarh	Haryana	778
Mansa	Punjab	782	Rewari	Haryana	784
Bathinda	Punjab	785	Samba	J&K	787
Kapurthala	Punjab	785	Sonipat	Haryana	790
Sangrur	Punjab	786	Jammu	J&K	794
Gurdaspur	Punjab	789	Beed	Maharashtra	800
Kurukshetra	Haryana	771	Ambala	Haryana	806
Ambala	Haryana	782	Rohtak	Haryana	807
Sonipat	Haryana	788	Pithoragarh	Uttarakhand	812

Source: Census of India, 2001 and 2011.

Table 2 shows that in 2001 Census, the bottom 10 districts in CSR fall in the two prosperous states of Punjab and Haryana. In 2001 Census, Fatehgarh Sahib in Punjab had the lowest CSR (766). In 2011 Census, some new districts like Jhajjar in Haryana topped the list of lowest CSR, followed by Mahendergarh and Rewari. In 2001 Census, these districts had the highest CSR. Samba in Jammu and Kashmir, Beed in Maharashtra and Pithoragarh in Uttarakhand joined the ranks of bottom 10 districts.

Sex Ratio at Birth

Sex ratio at birth is an important indicator displaying the plight of girl child. If we look at the sex ratio at birth, we find that at world level, the normal sex ratio at birth (SRB) is about

105 males per 100 females. The normal sex ratios at birth are found to lie between 943 and 971 females per thousand males. Accordingly, the normal figures for SRB are 953 females per thousand male children (Retherford and Roy, 2003; Arnold et al., 2002). In India, the normal SRB is worked out as female births per thousand males, which come out to 950, i.e. a normal SRB. On the contrary, what is worrisome is the fact that the sex ratio at birth has been declining in India and many states and there are big gaps between male and female births. This is further substantiated by NFHS reports over time shown in the table given below:

Table 3

Sex Ratio at Birth for the Major States

India and States	*NFHS–1 (92–93)*	*NFHS–2 (98–99)*	*NFHS–3 (05–06)*
India	951	935	920
Haryana	881	849	756
Punjab	876	860	728
Maharashtra	942	904	860
Tamil Nadu	1,021	946	930
Kerala	1,010	929	902
Delhi	926	828	848

Source: National Family and Health Surveys–1, 2, and 3.

The NFHS-based sex ratios at birth show a sharp decline in SRB not only in India but other states as well except Delhi, where there is some increase in SRB in NFHS–3. Punjab has the lowest SRB (728), followed by Haryana and Maharashtra. Surprisingly, Kerala too has seen a consistent decline in SRB as indicated in NFHS reports.

Field Setting

The present paper is based on an ethnographic study entitled 'Declining Child Sex Ratio and the Girl Child' conducted in Punjab and Haryana. In Punjab, the district of Fatehgarh

Sahib (rural-urban) was selected. In Haryana, the study was carried out in district Rohtak (rural-urban). An attempt has been made to explain how the family plans and uses discrete strategies to limit the family size, deciding the number of children particularly sons and daughters in the family. Why daughters have always been dispensed with and sons though considered essential, their number in the family is again not unlimited? Keeping in view these questions, the paper aims to examine some crucial issues such as values attached to boys and girls, dispensability of daughters, indispensability of sons, and strategies to plan families with at least one son.

Son Preference and Small Family Norm

It has been observed that during the past couple of years, there is a clear shift from traditional to modern idea of small family size. The success of family planning programme is seen in how seriously the message of two-child norm has articulated across different sections of society. In order to control the growth rate of population, the family planning programme was launched vigorously to reduce the fertility rate and right to abortion under certain conditions was legalized. With the result, unwanted and unplanned pregnancies were being terminated under Medical Termination of Pregnancies Act (MTP Act, 1971) without having any guilt whatsoever. With more and more medicalization of births, sonography and ultrasound checks are common; the desirable family now means 'two-child' family and that too of one's choice, i.e. family with at least one son and preferably without daughters and certainly not more than one daughter. The 'two-child' family norm coupled with the indiscriminate use of sex-selective technologies played havoc, imbalancing an all-time low sex ratio in general and child sex ratio in particular. A village doctor in rural Haryana said that family planning programme emphasizing small size of family is also responsible for foeticide.

Daughter discrimination and son preference have a long history and there are conscious and not so conscious strategies to plan families with sons and preferably without daughters. Preference for 'son' has deep roots for socio-cultural and economic reasons in Indian society. 'Since daughters leave after marriage and become permanent members of in-laws' family, therefore they are treated as "outgoing", having little economic value. Sons on the other hand are counted as "incoming" and permanent members of the family as they are supposed to support their ageing parents, continue family name and observe many rituals particularly after-death rituals of parents in the patriarchal society. Investment on them is counted as important as it pays off', as told by elderly women during a group discussion. It is also observed during the survey that birth of a male child is a decisive factor determining the family size. Large families have more daughters particularly among poor households. Many women opined that had their first child been a son, they would not have gone for a second child. Small families have either equal sex ratio of children or all sons/son. For some, one daughter is alright but two daughters cannot be tolerated.

Agrarian Economy and One-Son Family

Another significant observation is that since both the sites have agrarian economies, therefore land is a very precious asset. The fragmentation of land size into equal parts among the brothers has put enormous pressure on the dominant agricultural communities to have fewer children. Earlier survey on adverse sex ratio study (2008) conducted in Haryana (Rohtak) showed that people preferred smaller families with two boys and one girl. Two sons were required to continue the family name, with one son farming and the other one taking up some government job. As one woman put it, 'Having only son means a one-eyed person so what to see and what not to see.' Certainly the third son was not wished for at all. In Punjab, the choice for sons is not unlimited; one-son family is considered complete and need for a daughter is not being articulated. While boys continue to be the preferred sex, more than one son is not desired at all particularly in contemporary Punjab. One of the important reasons for not having more than one son in Punjab was with regard to preventing property division among sons. Among Jats, there was evidence of several families with only one child – a son. Now, the situation has changed in Haryana too, according to an ethnographic survey conducted recently (2011). Like Punjab, just one son is wished for to complete the family and need for a daughter is not being articulated. One of the important reasons to have just one son is to save further division of already small landholding as stated by a young husband and wife from Jat caste. In some villages, there are at least 10–12 households which have just one son and the women have already undergone tubectomy to avoid conception. It shows how conscious people are about the material conditions and living standard and this phenomenon of one-son family like we have in Punjab is fast catching up in Haryana too. Though sons are necessary, their number in the family is not unlimited. A village doctor in rural Haryana categorically mentioned that in landed families, the young married men have become so smart that they want to have just one son only to avoid the division of land. High cost of living, investments in education, dowry and upbringing of both boys and girls were cited as significant reasons for not having more than one son/daughter. It shows that to protect and conserve scarce household resources, people make discrete decisions to limit family size with son/s only at the cost of daughters (Sen, 1990; Coale, 1991).

Sex-Selective Technology and Use of Herbal Potions

Sociologists and demographers have often argued that sex selection takes place wherever there is a sharp fertility decline, with continued son preference and access to technologies and unregulated/illegal abortion services. Several studies have categorically pointed out the relationship between low sex ratio and prosperity, pointing to the killing role of technology in enhancing the missing girl phenomena. This is quite evident that technology is facilitating 'sex-preference', leading to elimination of the girl children even before birth. Surprisingly, this trend is spreading all over India. So, now what is happening is that there is an unholy alliance between tradition (son complex) and technology which is playing havoc with the society at large (Premi, 2001; Bose, 2001; Agnihotri, 2000).

In the field settings, the prevalence of sex-selective abortions was very well documented in all the sites; whether rich or poor; developed or under-developed, despite PNDT (Pre-natal Diagnostics Techniques; Regulation and Prevention of Misuse Act, 1994) and PCPNDT (Pre-conception and Pre-natal Diagnostic Technique; Prohibition of Sex Selection Act, 2003), sex-selective abortions continue unabated. In both rural and urban sites, in villages and towns, small families are preferred and this is deliberately done through de-selecting daughters. Both Punjab and Haryana reveal a particular situation where affluent and educated households across caste lines use the sex-selective technologies particularly in second order birth onwards to plan the family size. There is a clear shift towards a more conscious use of modern technologies of sex determination and sex selection.

To ensure the male child, it was observed that people in all the sites visit 'deras', 'maths' and seek the blessings of gurus/babas to have a male child. There are many cases of couples across caste and class lines using 'herbal potions' to confirm male child right at the time of first conception and later on abort the female foetus. It has been reported that in a large number of women who had taken such potions, the pregnancy culminated in miscarriages or still-births or in some cases children were born with defects. Desire for son is so intense that despite congenital defects, nothing is stopping people from using these potions to have a male child (John et al., 2008).

Even if couples have availed of herbal potions/blessings of holy men, surety is guaranteed only by the 'machine'.

Modern technology is an acceptable method to engineer size and composition. Abortion is also accepted as a mode of limiting family size, enable spacing and regulating sex composition of the family. A woman from Punjab stated, 'Today's women do not have to make guesses. Ultrasound is the biggest of all guesses. You can get the clear report. Get your ultrasound done and you know what is there.' Here, ultrasound technology is explicitly sought for sex determination. Ultrasound is considered to provide the 'practical solution' to the 'problem' of girl children and one which obviates moral dilemmas. The respondents from Punjab and Haryana admitted having undergone multiple abortions sometimes as many as 6–8 times after a daughter till she had a son – such examples abound and people know that sex-selective abortion is a crime. People know about such 'popular clinics' that are named openly as being popular providers of testing and abortion services. Small towns have become hubs for surrounding villages and small towns. To confirm the sex of the baby, a middle-aged woman who already had a daughter accompanied her mother and went to 'a nursing home' in Sirhind, which charged ₹ 7,000. But she was not satisfied and got an ultrasound test done the second time to ensure a male baby. She further told that had there been a daughter again, she would have aborted it because she and her husband did not want to have two daughters at any cost. On female foeticide, a woman in Rohtak (rural) said, 'Till a male child is not born, killing female child is not a murder. If it is, then everyone is doing it. Now everyone gets a son by abortion only.' Girls are considered a burden because one has to spend on their education and dowry. Pressure of the in-laws, particularly mother-in-law, is also responsible for foeticide. Despite the fact that there is worldwide concern for the decline in sex ratio, people are not bothered; rather, they plan families as per their choice, i.e. selecting son at the cost of daughter.

There are many cases where women have undergone sex determination tests to confirm the sex of the baby and subsequently led to abortions if it is a female foetus. When women were asked about the tensions during pregnancy, most of them replied that 'they are bothered about the sex of the baby even in the first pregnancy because if it is a son then there is no need to go for the second child.' But tensions mount manifold during second pregnancy, especially if the first child is a daughter and no one wished to have a second daughter at all. It was also observed that affluent people resorted to technological interventions early in their fertility careers while poorer people did so later or simply regretted that they could not do so due to lack of financial means. Neglect then becomes the default option. The costs of such tests varied across the sites. Sometimes tests were needed several times. Despite knowledge of sex determination being an offence, and despite higher costs, couples are continuing to resort to it and justifying abortion.

As regards the expenditure on ultrasound and abortion, it is not counted as wasteful; rather, it is viewed in the context of savings by having a small family especially if there is no girl. Despite PNDT and PCPNDT, the use of ultrasound is found to be rampant, with doctors, nurses, ANMs and other medical personnel benefiting monetarily. Women in both the sites knew the places where ultrasound tests were carried out by doctors and para-medical staff in clinics and centres in Sirhind, Patiala, Karnal, Sonepat, Panipat, Jhajjar, Rohtak and Delhi. There are direct and indirect pressures on women to produce male heirs. The woman not only feels ashamed of producing a girl child, but also loses her worth and regains it only after giving birth to sons. If she does not comply, the repercussions can be desertion, bringing a co-wife, physical, mental and emotional ill-treatment. It infers that during the last two decades, with the advent of new sex-selective technologies, it is now easier for people to decide the elimination of girl child at an early stage. What is happening now is the replacement of age-old practice of killing daughters with pre-birth elimination with the help of medical technologies.

Dispensability of Daughters and Indispensability of Sons

Despite the fact that girls are eliminated, positive values are attached to the girl child in both the field sites irrespective of rural-urban residence. People expressed positive values for daughters mainly because girls bring discipline in the family; they are very close to parents and take care; kinship continues only with girls; relationships are extended further by marrying girls. A voice from rural Punjab explains mother's love and affection for the daughter: 'Girls are their mother's favourites. When girls grow up, they become friends to their mothers.' On the contrary, strong resentment was shown for boys as they indulge in over-spending, addiction, eve-teasing, bring a bad name to the family, are not serious in studies and career building, etc. In Fatehgarh Sahib in Punjab, people were very categorical about 'worthless sons' where unemployment and drug addiction are taking their toll on an entire generation of young men.

Though people valued girl child, they showed a strong dislike for having her as expressed by a large number of women during field work. They openly maintained that girls are not at all wanted because of various reasons. Most of them said, 'We cannot afford to have a daughter as she is very expensive. She has to be given huge dowry." An elderly Jat Sikh woman from an agricultural joint family stressed quite emphatically that her family could not afford to have a girl because of small landholding. 'Marriage of girl requires a lot of money to be spent on dowry. A poor family cannot bear the burden. Due to economic constraints, we do not want to have daughters,' she said.

Some of the women expressed that they would not like to have a daughter because of insecurity and over-protection, while others said that daughter is not a burden but if she is 'unfortunate', unlucky or 'destiny' is against her, then the whole family suffers. Some of them said that bearing of daughter means ill-treatment of woman by in-laws. It lowers her status in the family. Another voice from urban Rohtak reveals the helplessness of a woman for not giving birth to a daughter due to societal pressures as she herself feels the pangs of being a woman. She told that the taunts that she has borne over the years have forced her to abort female foetus as girls are considered a burden on the family. They face violence inside and outside family. She very categorically stressed that it is better to die than giving birth to a daughter.

During group discussions held in rural Punjab and Haryana in which young girls and women of all age groups participated, it was observed that all of them stated very categorically that 'without a girl', the family can manage but 'without a son', the family cannot manage at all. Such cases show the darker side of otherwise prosperous Punjab and Haryana. If anything wrong happens with the girl or if she is ill-treated by her in-laws, her parents have no way out or power to tackle the problem. It also shows 'what it means to be a parent of a daughter'. It is sheer parents' helplessness that forces them not to have daughters. Another problem listed here is the increasing greed for dowry. Addiction among youth is so pervasive in Punjab that it becomes difficult for parents to select a perfect match for their daughters. People are overwhelmingly bothered about the addiction of young boys who do nothing and create nuisance everywhere.

Between sons and daughters, it is the daughters who are more dispensable and vulnerable and are therefore being killed. In Punjab and Haryana, though more sons in the family are not welcomed, they are neither killed nor neglected. With regard to the worth of daughter and daughter-in-law, it was observed that it is the woman not the daughter who gains importance to run the family. Women are mainly required to produce and reproduce for the family and their roles are taken over by daughters-in-law when they grow old. This is the reason that daughters are valued but not worth having and without daughter-in-law, the house is incomplete as she is the bearer of sons and perpetuates the patriarchal social order.

Aversion to daughters has to be seen with rising age of marriage resulting in more expenditure on education, health, marriage and dowry. Due to the practice of hypergamy–a feature in which the status of bride giver is lower than the bride taker – girls are married in better status families implying more bowing down, giving expensive gifts to boy and his family, elaborate and lavish marriages particularly when the groom is better educated and holding a good government job. Daughters continue to be looked upon as 'outgoings' rather than 'incomings' and hence the focus is on not having them at all.

Non-Marriage of Men

Scarcity of brides in contemporary Punjab and Haryana is a serious implication of skewed child sex ratio leading to non-marriage of young men. Since girls are already lesser in number and better educated, therefore families look for better placed boys, preferably urban, resulting in squeezing of marriage cohort (Ahlawat, 2009). No one would like to marry his/her daughter to a person who does not earn for himself and the family. One of the serious implications of the skewed sex ratio is reflected in 'male marriage squeeze'. To cope with the situation, men across caste lines are bringing brides from distant states like Uttarakhand, Bihar, Jharkhand, West Bengal, Maharashtra, North–East and even Kerala. These women are brought from across cultural, regional and language contexts where caste and sometimes even religion is different (Kaur, 2004).

Conclusion and Suggestions

Despite Central and state governments' initiatives in the form of various schemes and programmes to strengthen the girl child, enactment of PCPNDT Act (1994, amended 2003) to check the unscrupulous use of sex determination technologies, role of media to sensitize the society at large through reporting on girl child deficit and sustained efforts and campaign of civil society organizations and activists, nothing seems to be working to stop discrimination against the girl child. Rather, the nexus between doctors, nurses, ANMs and other medical, para-medical personnel is flourishing into a big business deal. However, both the 2001 and the 2011 Census reports have clearly shown that the implementation of the PCPNDT Act has been tardy as there is a further decline in child sex ratio.

It is high time to create awareness among different stakeholders and the community at large about the negative impact of declining child sex ratio on society. It is equally important to empower women to create gender just society whereby women take the responsibility of their ageing parents, which reduces dependence on sons. There is a need to create an environment where daughters too are natural heirs of parental property so that they are independent and do not have to rely on others for their needs. It is equally important to involve girls to perform rituals over sons at parent's funeral and all after-death rituals. Religious leaders have a great role to play by discouraging discrimination against the girl child, stopping sex determination tests and female foeticide. There is a strong need to have proper implementation and monitoring of PCPNDT Act at different levels.

References

Agnihotri, Satish Balram. 2000. *Sex Ratio Patterns in the Indian Population: A Fresh Exploration*, New Delhi: Sage Publications.

Ahlawat, N. 2009. 'Missing Brides in Rural Haryana', *Social Change*, Vol. 39, No. 1, March, pp. 46–63.

Arnold, F., S. Kishor and T.K. Roy. 2002. 'Sex Selective Abortions in India', *Population and Development Review*, Vol. 28, No. 4, pp. 759–85.

Bose, A. 2001. *India's Billion Plus People: 2001 Census Highlights, Methodology and Media Coverage*, New Delhi: B.R. Publishing Corporation.

Coale, Ansley J. 1991. 'Excess Female Mortality and the Balance of the Sexes in the Population: An Estimate of the Number of Missing Females', *Population and Development Review*, Vol. 17, No. 3, pp. 517–23.

Dasgupta, M. 1987. 'Selective Discrimination Against Female Children in Rural Punjab, India', *Population and Development Review*, Vol. 13, No. 1, pp. 77–100.

——. 2005. 'Explaining Asia's Missing Women: A New Look at the Data', *Population and Development Review*, Vol. 31, No. 3, pp. 529–35.

John, Mary E., Ravinder Kaur, Rajni Palriwala, Saraswati Raju and Alpana Sagar. 2008. *Planning Families, Planning Gender: The Adverse Child Sex Ratio in Selected Districts of Punjab, Haryana, Himachal Pradesh, Rajasthan and Madhya Pradesh*, Bangalore: Books for Change.

Kaur, Ravinder. 2004. 'Across Region Marriages: Poverty, Female Migration and Sex Ratio', *Economic and Political Weekly*, Vol. XXXIX, No. 25, pp. 2595–602.

Miller, Barbara D. 1981. *The Endangered Sex: Neglect of Female Children in Rural North India*, Ithaca: Cornell University Press.

Minturn, Leigh. 1993. *Sita's Daughters: Coming Out of Purdah*, New Delhi: Oxford University Press.

Mitra, Asok. 2001. 'Implication of Declining Sex Ratio in India in Enduring Conundrum: India's Sex Ratio', in Vina Mazumdar and N. Krishnaji (eds), *Essays in Honour of Asok Mitra*, Delhi: Rainbow, pp. 143–98.

Premi, M.K. and S. Raju. 1996. 'Imbalance in Child Sex Ratio in Madhya Pradesh, Unpublished Report', Sponsored by Ministry of Human Resource Development, Government of India.

Premi, M.K. 2001. 'The Missing Girl Child', *Economic and Political Weekly*, Vol. 36, No. 21, pp. 1875–80.

Retherford, Robert D. and T.K. Roy. 2003 'Factors Affecting Sex Selective Abortions in 17 Major States', National Family Health Survey Reports, Number 21, International Institute for Population Sciences, Mumbai, India, East-West Center Program on Population, Honolulu, Hawaii, USA.

Sen, Amartya. 1990. 'More than 100 Million Women are Missing', *New York Review of Books*, Vol. 37, No. 20, December, pp. 61–66.

Sudha, S. and S. Irudaya Rajan. 1999. 'Female Demographic Disadvantage in India, 1991: Sex Selective Abortions and Female Infanticide, 1981–1991', *Development and Change*, Vol. 30, No. 2, pp. 585–61.

Vishwanath, I.S. 2004. 'Female Infanticide: The Colonial Experience', *Economic and Political Weekly*, 29 May, pp. 2313–18.

5

Women and the Conservative Backlash in Society and Media

Manjeet Rathee

Neo-liberal reform in the era of globalization promises rapid entry into modernity for so-called 'Third World' countries lagging behind in developmental indicators. The changes it brings about are not confined to the economic level; to fulfil its agenda, it has to effect simultaneous changes in the polity, in modes of governance, in social norms and practices and in the ideological and cultural sphere. It also needs to be in control of various agencies, such as the system of education, media, the family, the community and the like through which the consent of the people to these radical reforms can be ensured. All these social institutions and practices have to be 'modernized' so as to become the bearers of its ideological influence. The rapid technical revolutions in print and electronic media in the last two decades in particular have been seen as the epitome of such modernization; through these we are supposed to have broken communication barriers and been tagged with global media. It has been possible to get rid of the compulsions of government control of media and attain a certain degree of autonomy guided by the principle of self-regulation; print media has proliferated through digitization and satellite technology and there are now hundreds of private news and entertainment channels on television too from which to pick and choose. Same is the case with FM channels on radio. Sheer rapidity of communication, shiny packaging and a general ambience of 'free for all' that one finds today in media are highlighted as sure signs of globalized modernity. Its power and spread are also supposed to have an influence on our social mores and our aspirations through which we may be propelled into global economy.

Yet, in these last two decades, there has been an unprecedented rise in caste-based, communal, fundamentalist and patriarchal ideology in our country as also a shrinking of secular democratic spaces in society and in media. The 'conservative backlash' referred to in the title brings all this together so that they reinforce one another and breed irrationality and superstition, that has an adverse impact on all remaining democratic spaces in society. National Crime Record Bureau (NCRB) data tell us that recorded crimes against women have grown at an exponential rate during this time; the growth rate is even higher if one calculates it from the 1970s. There has been a whopping 10 times increase in rape cases from 1971 to 2012 with 2,487 incidents of rape in 1971 to 24,923 cases in 2012 (Source: NCRB, 2012). This can be only partially explained by the fact that the rate of such crimes being recorded has grown. There can be no doubt that there has also been a real increase. Dowry-related violence, the overwhelming desire for sons leading to elimination of the girl child, the slave-like exploitation of women and children through trafficking are all examples of age-old crimes associated with a retrograde patriarchal ideology. But all these practices find 'modern' means of perpetuating and strengthening themselves in today's market society. Electronic and print media as representational modes, for all their profession of modernity, very often embody and reinforce the same retrograde values. Since entertainment gets equated with mindless consumption and information itself gets presented as 'infotainment', the owners of media do not mind promoting retrograde and skewed values if they are 'entertaining' enough.

The aggressive conservative tendencies that one finds today both in society and in media are not mere remnants of earlier times; they are different from a passive lingering over backdated values and mores. The violent resurgence of casteist, communal and patriarchal trends today is inextricably related to neo-liberal culture of which it is part and parcel. Neo-liberal culture, which represents the hegemonic power of world capitalism today, often uses aggressive conservatism to assert its control over people's minds and although the connections may not be immediately evident, the linkages between the two can, in no way, be denied.

In any traditional society, whenever the forces of social change are at work, all the well-known patriarchal institutions are up in arms against it because gender relations are in the cusp of such change and social control over all groups subordinated by patriarchy are perceived as being endangered. In the 19th century, when the country had been under colonial domination, issues like women's education, widow remarriage and the like had been regarded by the conservative forces in society as signs of *kaliyuga* turning social relations topsy-turvy and encouraging sinful ways. The British state was reluctant to meddle with practices like 'sati' and child-marriage, but under pressure from a strong reform movement from within society, it moved in to make the legal changes that could counter such practices.

Today, we have a Constitution as well as many legal provisions endorsing modern democratic values and gender equality. But the neo-liberal state allows the tirade against the values articulated in the Constitution and laws to continue with impunity. The tirade comes from powerful religious and social lobbies as also from right reactionary communal political forces which have had a resurgence in the last twenty years. Further, it comes from proponents of identity politics. Wherever women try to assert themselves and take a stand against social conservatism, the effort is denigrated as alien to our traditions and a result of rampant westernization. Any legal or social reform becomes suspect. Thus, even in the mid–1980s, when aggressive communalism was on the rise, both the protest against the 'sati' of Rup Kanwar in Deorala and the support of the Supreme Court's award of maintenance to Shah Bano were attacked by fundamentalists of different hues as violating religious traditions. These were ploys on both sides to mobilize women on religious lines to aim a blow at any united women's movement for progressive reforms. Oppressed by social conservatism as they are, women nonetheless often tend to internalize these campaigns and it becomes more difficult for them to resist the system.

In more recent times, so-called 'gurus' and 'sants', who have amassed wealth and power on the basis of religious pretensions, brazenly announce that women expose themselves as targets of rapists by going out freely and by rejecting conservative ways of dress and deportment. One often hears remarks from some of the high-ranking administrators and bureaucrats blaming modernization of women rather than the administration that fails to protect them for rapes. In the recent debates on the anti-rape law, both within and outside Parliament, many voices were heard which looked at rape as a crime against women's 'chastity' and 'modesty' and not as an attack on her dignity and integrity as a person. A lawyer defending the accused in the 'Nirbhaya' case said in a public outburst that if his daughter went out at night with a man not related to her, he would burn her alive (*The Times of India*, 14 September 2013)! Senior parliamentarians were found cracking jokes about 'stalking' being a natural male instinct during the debate in the House. Such retrograde positions are by no means limited to reactionary forces or individuals, but similar tirades are sometimes heard even from those professing liberal ideology. The Justice Verma Committee Report (2013) asks the agonized question: why is it that neither the Government nor the Parliament comes up loud and clear to say that the 'khap panchayats' committing crimes of every kind are illegal and unconstitutional and must be suppressed (*Report of the Committee on Amendments to Criminal Law,* 2013: 32)? This is because even professedly liberal forces in them have turned defensive against the reactionary onslaught and are acting not out of courage of conviction, but only with narrow political ends in view.

The manner in which the minimum 'age of consent' was raised in the latest anti-rape law (2013) shows that this backlash feeds on unabashed moral authoritarianism. Many organizations in the country today are thriving on this platform of extreme moral authoritarianism which often culminates in vicious physical attacks on their targets. Armed goons are mobilized for acts of vandalism which are given a high moral colouring. These reactionary groups are also notorious for their attacks on young people for exercising their choice in various significant matters related to their lives, particularly for their crusades against inter-caste marriages by young people. Such groups also spread the myth of a 'love jihad', according to which Muslim boys are deliberately trained in methods meant to seduce Hindu girls. The campaign of 'Bahu beti bachao', which precipitated the recent riots in Muzaffarnagar, gains its momentum from such myths. While inciting communal feelings, this campaign actually derives its potency from the patriarchal fear of losing control over the women of the community and the belief that this moral policing holds society together. The state itself shows the same hypocritical attitude of moral policing in Maharashtra when it closes down dance bars for spreading social corruption, throwing many dancing girls from poor families out of their livelihood. The moot point here is that instead of offering the women some protection in their work or some less exploitative option in livelihood, this moral policing by the state makes them even more vulnerable to sexual exploitation than before. In fact, as the neo-liberal state policy deprives the vast majority of the people from their basic rights of food, shelter, education and work, all the values of modern democracy protecting these rights are trashed as incompatible with our traditions and coercive conservatism becomes an essential part of dominant ideology.

Retrograde ideas regarding gender are strengthened by communal and caste-based campaigns. In all cases of caste-based and communal violence even in the past, women of the 'other' caste or community have always been targets of attack. There have been most heinous attacks on women from minority and backward caste communities in various parts of the country to take revenge for protecting the 'honour' of a particular caste or community. In a most recent incident, a teenage tribal girl from Birbhum district of West Bengal was 'punished' by the community for wanting to marry a person of another caste by 'ordering' a gang rape against her by her own acquaintances. In the last two decades of neo-liberal polity and society, there has been a resurgence of such incidents.

Justifying caste violence in the name of 'tradition', particularly when women are the targets of it, also goes on with impunity. These incidents are often projected as punishment for women who are perceived as having challenged 'rules' laid down by society such as not entering temples, not using water from a particular well and so on. Only a few years back, Kherlaunji in Maharashtra witnessed the rape and killing of women from a Dalit family because they were perceived as not having been sufficiently submissive. A local court in Rajasthan in 1992 gave the verdict in the case of Bhanwari Devi that the upper caste accused were senior respectable people and it would be impossible for them by their very nature to lead a sexual assault on a woman from the lower caste. Even the judiciary is not free from reactionary prejudices with which sentences passed by them are inflected.

These retrogressive outbreaks in society should have been kept under control by a democratic, secular state pledged to the ideal of equality but this is not being done. In fact, the neo-liberal state is itself becoming more vitiated by communal and ethnic chauvinism of which we may find ample examples in regions under Armed Forces Special Powers Act and elsewhere. The rape and murder of Manorama in Manipur, the mass rape by Army personnel of the women of Kunan-Poshpora in Kupwara in Kashmir, or the so-called 'encounter' killing of the young Ishrat Jahan in Gujarat show how the state itself is acting in a way inimical to democracy, putting whole communities or ethnic groups at the receiving end of punishments meant to put an end to terrorism. This only helps to nurture the growth of conservative aggression also in the social fabric, leading to the proliferation of violence both within and among castes, communities and ethnic groups, and women are exposed to both kinds of violence.

While inter-caste and inter-community violence forms one side of the context in which conservative backlash grows apace, the other side of this context is multiplication of women's oppression within groups and communities as a result of identity politics. In the name of caste or communal identity, women within a particular social group are marked as the property of that group and subjected to more and more stringent restrictions; any deviation is severely punished. This typically represents a backward pull away from modern democratic values as greater mobility of women in a changing world is seen as a danger. Women getting educated or going out to work are tolerated only so long as these activities do not clash with norms imposed by the community. It is not that the competitive, consumerist market society of present times is rejected as a whole by the community, but it is felt that the adverse effects of the change can be contained only if those who are under subjection, including women, remain under subjection, if social hierarchies are maintained. Hence, customs which are skewed against women and have lost their relevance are being revived.

The minorities, and even groups that have been socially marginalized, also show an ingrowing, parochial tendency in oppressing their women. The *fatwa* delivered less than a decade ago in the case of Imrana in Uttar Pradesh who had been raped by her father-in-law, so that, being a woman, she would be paying for the crime perpetrated on her, shows how within minority communities too, the conservative backlash operates against women. More often, this expresses itself in the form of rulings against use of mobile phones by women, of dress codes such as observing 'hijab' and also of course in ruling out choice in marriage in the case of daughters. These tendencies are found among ethnic minorities too. In some North–eastern states, customary laws on property and representation in local councils which exclude women have recently got a new lease of life. The fact that the Hindu Right has appropriated the call for a Uniform Civil Code on the claim that the reformed Hindu Code should be the model for Uniform Civil Code, has roused suspicions of a majoritarian co-option and has made it difficult to renew the discourse. But unless gender-exclusive customary laws are dropped or changed to make them more equal for women, the conservative forces within the community will be strengthened.

But the greatest threat that identity politics presents to women's equality is in the immense extra-constitutional power enjoyed today by 'Khap Panchayats', 'Caste Panchayats' and now 'Maha Panchayats' in defiance of the norms of a modern democratic state. There are calls from certain retrograde sections from within both Hindu and Muslim communities to lower the minimum age of marriage. Khap Panchayats go several steps further to impose penalties on couples who have married by choice for having violated the 'honour' of the community. An eminent woman politician of Punjab, convicted for detention and enforced abortion (though not for murder) of her daughter who died an unnatural death apparently for 'honour', continues to enjoy immense prestige as a religious leader within her community. If a social leader behaves in this fashion, it is no wonder that very recently in Garnawati, Rohtak, in Haryana, a father after having brutally massacred his daughter and her husband, made a statement to the effect that what he had done was right and anybody wanting to uphold the honour of the family would have done the same. The worst effects of the conservative backlash then may be seen as being visited on the younger generation, who expect the benefits of equality and democracy from the state.

It has already been pointed out that within the legislature, the executive and the judiciary, which are various arms of the state, there seem to be definite reactionary trends over which there is little control. One of the most shocking examples of the erosion of a democratic vision may be found in the fact that several times since 1996, the Government and the Parliament have failed to enact the Women's Reservation Bill, which would amend the Constitution to allow women 33 per cent reservation in Parliament and in state assemblies. It has been resisted on grounds that 'qualified' women in sufficient numbers shall not be found and only urban elite women 'with short hair' will benefit. For some time now, a powerful misogynist lobby of 'endangered males' has been very active in the corridors of power against certain laws which were passed after decades of movement by women's organizations to give women some protection from domestic violence. These are Section 498A of IPC and Protection of Women from Domestic Violence Act (2005). Women's organizations know from their experience on the ground that most cases of marital and domestic abuse never come to the police or the courts of law, and the procedures being long and complicated, very few women are able to get justice or to secure conviction even when they take recourse to law. But these lobbies raise a hue and cry over misuse of such laws demanding that they be withdrawn or diluted. The shocking thing is that the Central Government, as also a section of the judiciary, without any understanding of what happens at the ground level, chooses to be swayed by this campaign. Either through Government orders or judicial verdicts, laws to protect women from marital and domestic abuse are toned down. Those who are in power do not seem to be seriously inclined either to bring in laws where necessary to protect and expand the democratic rights of the people, or to implement strongly and comprehensively laws which already exist. Even after the new Criminal Law Amendment Act (2013), horrendous incidents of sexual assault continue without fear of reprisal. The conservative backlash takes advantage of this hiatus in governance.

In the last couple of decades, there has been a 'corporatization' of religion as of many social institutions. Religious spaces like temples, mosques, festivals and rituals which had earlier been more amorphous in their organization, are now being taken over by big money and being developed as professional profitable enterprises. These are also appearing as spectacles on media and being further legitimized. Even in our education system, side by side with growing privatization and commercialization, the new economy promotes all kinds of superstitions, gender-insensitive approaches and communally divisive inputs in the name of value-education. The result of this is that even as citizenship rights are eliminated through neo-liberal reforms, a substitute space for mobilization is offered through superstitious practices and rituals supported by big money and highlighted in corporate media. Education, to the extent that it is increasingly encroached upon by retrograde ideologies, does not protect us against this. The security and dignity that is no more available to the people as citizens seems now to inhere in integration with religious or social community, as Hindus, as Muslims, as members of a particular powerful caste or 'khap', as devotees of this or that 'guru' who appears on a particular channel to provide succour from alienation and deep isolation.

In the neo-liberal dispensation, this fragmentation of the ethics of equality serves the interest of aggressive capitalism; but it leads inevitably to the proliferation of superstitions and unreason and of a coercive ethos. In the present economic order, identification and elimination of the girl child within the womb by using advanced technology thrives as big business; but what is significant is that doctors, trained in and equipped with such technology, generally justify this by referring to the traditional demand for sons and by reinforcing this demand. As the market casts women in new stereotypes as consumers, dowry also gets subsumed under this market and its status as a powerful family tradition is reinforced by the market which profits from the exchange of various assets and consumer goods that ostensibly enhance the status of the bride. On the other hand, in the unorganized labour market, women working within/for/outside families are still rooted in their older traditional roles and therefore remain producers or providers of services in lieu of low wages. Their rights as labourers can be denied on this basis. There is no equality in work under neo-liberal dispensation. Greater freedom and greater mobility for working women is being touted, but when it comes to working conditions, they remain deprived as inferior and partial workers who ideally should have stayed at home. The conservative backlash against women's rights therefore is very much in the interest of neo-liberal reform.

There has also been resistance and consistent struggle against this re-emergence of aggressive conservatism. Starting from the 1980s, when communal politics was on the rise and gender became one of the focal points of its attack, many progressive, liberal-minded and democratic groups have waged a battle against dowry, against the Muslim Women's Protection Bill, the glorification of 'sati' and other issues related to retrogressive ideology and mindset. These groups have launched joint campaigns, brought out booklets, organized discussions and have mobilized women from different walks of life in protest against such resurgence. These protest measures have sometimes forced the government and the administration to take reluctant steps in bringing justice to women. These groups have played a crucial role in the struggle for equal laws and for their implementation. Whether it is laws against dowry, domestic violence, sexual assault or harassment of women at workplace, or a law against 'honour' crimes, democratic and secular forces have made positive interventions and helped in the preparation and implementation of laws at every stage. It is imperative to organize more sustained campaigns on existing laws supporting women's rights and provide legal support for women who are trying to resist the conservative backlash, while continuing the campaign for laws on women's reservation, honour crimes, marital property rights and reproductive technologies.

With the opening up of our economy to profit-oriented global market forces, representation of women in both print and electronic media and in the advertisement industry has gone through a makeover. Two broad trends can easily be discerned – either women are commoditized aggressively as sex objects for the sale of various products where in the name of modernity, the entire worth and identity of women is reduced to graphic and titillating representation of their body, or alternately, they are depicted in traditional stereotyped roles as 'ideal' wife or mother or 'bahu' confined to the boundaries of homes and hearths. This could be seen in the 'proud' display of their domestic subjugation or the whole range of 'saas-bahu' serials in the name of family drama, or the portrayal of different categories of working women trying to entice or please their bosses in different ways solely by exploiting their bodily charms for promotion, marriage or other prospects. This tendentious reconstruction of reality into a world of conservative wish-fulfilment also makes women from different social positions and communities, engaged in confronting real life issues and problems, invisible in the world of media.

The 'visibility' of women has indeed increased on the small screen and in print media, but the 'status-quoist' and conservative images mostly represent upper middle class, Hindu high caste men and women dedicated to a lifestyle and ideology representing a patriarchal value system. Where minority communities are represented, insignia of religious identity are copiously present. Globalization in media has been widely advertised as having a liberating effect and offering freedom of choice. But in a world 'increasingly dominated by things and by consumption', the sole drive to sell and earn profit has only led to reinforcement and proliferation of discriminatory and exclusive images in the name of empowerment. In advertisements, the modern mother and housewife who sets the standards of consumption within the household or even the skimpily dressed young careerist woman, is not presented in an absolutely negative manner because they embody consumerist desires on which advertisements thrive, but in most serials a woman with a modern outlook and consciousness signifies undesirable qualities and is almost invariably either caricatured and derided or she is presented as arrogant and conceited, with little or no respect for family, human values or human relationships. Further, women's progressive struggles for equality and violence-free life are often trashed by presenting them as protests for objects like cosmetics or trivial family issues.

It has sometimes been argued that the deliberate foregrounding of the female body in electronic media represents aspirations of freedom from traditional stereotyping of the woman and strengthens modernity. There is no doubt that in advertisements, in particular, the display of the female body as signifying certain values often breaks with traditional representations in so far as dress codes, deportment, preoccupations and practices are concerned. They become visual icons of modernity in a certain sense. They are also presented as being able to make their own choices in all the areas mentioned above. But an in-depth look at such representations often shows that they too are generated by the exigencies of the 'male gaze' or by consumerist aspirations inspired by the market. They do not act as agents of change, but only promote a new set of stereotypes presented to the possible buyer of goods.

Majority of the television serials that are currently being broadcast do not have any relevance to the existing social realities and problems but only contribute to developing a desire for an 'extravagant lifestyle'. Contrary to the popular belief of being healthy family entertainers, they actually reinforce 'tensions within the family' because the majority of them deal with urban, successful and rich or middle class women who are almost always depicted as jealous, mean, and spoilt, constantly scheming and plotting against each other in an effort to become more 'powerful' and 'dictatorial' both at home and in public life. Even in serials dealing apparently with real social problems like child marriage, female foeticide, widowhood or caste oppression, the content and social messaging would reveal to an in-depth study a totally derogatory and negative portrayal of women in various roles – either a mother-in-law who turns into a 'monster-in-law' or a young girl becoming a widow and going through traumatic rituals again at the insistence of another woman, a girl child being shown as totally unacceptable and unwanted in the family or a young girl being castigated or even killed mercilessly for taking her own decisions. What popular serials usually do is to normalize such portrayals, emphasizing their inevitability.

Lifestyles and value systems depicted in these serials and advertisements have led to tremendous increase in expenses and ostentation at the time of marriage and other 'auspicious' occasions, religious festivals, etc. The glorification of expensive marriage gifts, huge sets where the ceremony is conducted, *mehandi*, *ladies sangeet* are setting a standard; the market intrudes into every 'family occasion' for the sale of its products. This is most brazenly seen in festivals and fasts related to women like *karwa chauth* and *dhanteras* which, thanks to aggressive promotion by the market, have even reached the eastern and the southern states where they had had no importance earlier. In advertisement after advertisement, the cash nexus is presented as the motive force in family and social relationships – be it husband-wife, parent-child or any other relationship. A particular brand of car or television, a particular cream, lotion or deodorant or even a brand of 'paan masala' is all that is needed in forging a bond between the two families or in choosing a husband or a wife. Festivals involving ritual fasts and *pooja*, or superstitious observances like *vaastu* have been worst exploited by the corporate media. One can find a host of channels propagating totally irrational customs and practices, all kinds of cures and remedies in the name of religion. The resurgence of faith in 'sadhus' and 'sadhvis' pretending to be 'saviours' or 'avatars' propagating false, anti-democratic, casteist and anti-secular beliefs has full support of many eminent members of the polity so that they keep on being highlighted by media. In the present deteriorating economic and social conditions, such media images exploit the multiple problems and agony of the people to enhance their own popularity and the wealth and influence of such fraudulent persons.

A proliferating beauty business, selling not just cosmetics and beauty treatments but dreams of empowerment, celebrity, happiness and love, influences even those who lack the power to buy them. Since advertising agencies believe that exceedingly slim and fair-skinned models sell products as well as set standards of modern looks and glamour, so all advertisements and serials on television aggressively highlight the importance of acquiring these qualities which alone can enhance the value of the users in a consumer society. In countless advertisements, we find that dark skin becomes a continuous source of anxiety and inferiority complex not only for the 'unfortunate' girl but for her parents and everyone around her as well. The use of a particular cream or whitening agent suddenly transforms her to 'magic fairness' and all her problems are instantly solved – be it marriage or a promotion or getting a good job in a multinational company. This unnecessary glorification of fair skin is against scientific principles concerning healthcare and not only promotes false notions of 'beauty' and 'superiority' based on skin tones and external appearance, but also revives at the same time the whole obnoxious discourse of racial discrimination. Moreover, all other human values get replaced by the obsession with 'things', the possession of which is supposed to be the ultimate insignia of worth. In the name of modernity and choice, this beauty business is seeking to make women victims of the market, manipulating their irrational desires and reconstructing their lives for its own purpose.

Such exclusive, superficial and demeaning representation of women in media pushes to the very margins of the world constructed by it the real life day-to-day experiences of the vast majority of ordinary women and poor, rural women, the complexities of whose struggle for survival and dignity media brushes aside with unconcern. Their struggles for education, for violence-free life, for more favourable conditions at the workplace only rarely succeed in getting represented in mainstream media although they concern the lived lives of the vast majority of women. When the identity of the women at the grassroots is 'essentialized' and 'homogenized' in whatever meagre images we find of them in media, the real issues of their lives become invisible. It is significant that the new market-based media that has been self-righteously proclaiming progress and freedom of opinions to be its goals can turn so oppressive and so tendentious where its own representations are concerned. It shows that, being controlled by big capital, it shares the exploitative character of the present neo-liberal economy. Hence, it is imperative that those who are involved in these struggles should, in their own campaigns, critically negotiate with the whole issue of modernity and empowerment as interpreted in the context of the worldwide operations of media and communication technology.

It is sometimes argued that media fulfils demands actually existing in society; that, in other words, media is 'giving the people what they want'. This is far from the truth. The fact of the matter is that corporate media is only interested in creating demand for its own products; it has a very strong vested interest in promoting and propagating conservatism and pseudo-modern representations of women and in ignoring the needs of the more disadvantaged sections of society. Corporate media does not only generate actual products, it also generates the demand for them. Market demand is falsely projected as public demand in order to continue with this discriminatory and exclusivist agenda. New demands construct new stereotypes and representation of women as aggressive consumers of objects of pleasure serves the dual purpose of subjugating and confining women to the new patriarchy of the market and at the same time, of making the pleasure of looking at the beautiful images of female bodies identical with the pleasure of looking at the saleable commodities. The attraction lies in the total package. The socializing powers of modern media are tremendous, but its potentials for disseminating more inclusive messages more sensitive to people's real needs are restricted by its being under the control of corporate capital. However, it is still necessary to use the contradictions within mainstream media – its proclamations of freedom of opinion and inclusiveness in opposition to its actual manipulative practices – to find spaces within it for other views and other voices to the extent possible. The question of public accountability also has to be raised whenever objectionable and harmful images and messages are projected through it. As a check to the dissemination of retrograde ideology by foregrounding demeaning images of women, a transparent and enabling Broadcasting Code needs to be put in place after consultation with all sections of the public. People, and women among them, have always communicated among themselves about their lives and struggles in many ways before the recent revolutions in electronic technology. All these alternative modes such as documentary films, theatre and other live performances, booklets, posters, conversations must be developed to counteract the dissemination of the conservative backlash through corporate media.

References

National Crime Record Bureau (NCRB). 2012. *Crimes in India: 2011 Statistics*, Government of India, New Delhi.

Singh, A.P. 2013. *The Times of India*, New Delhi, 14 September.

Verma, Justice J.S. 2013. *Report of the Committee on Amendments to Criminal Law*, Government of India, New Delhi.

6

Dispensing with Daughters

Exploring the Socio-Economic and Cultural Dimensions of Female Foeticide and Infanticide

Anjali Dewan

The girl children in India have been the most vulnerable for centuries and are, even today, vulnerable to the insults of deprivation as well as discrimination. Whatever the natural biological laws of human reproduction given to mankind for balancing its natural sex ratio have been taken away by man-made laws, customs, traditions, religious beliefs and sophisticated medical technology, resulting in a lower status in society for girls as well as women. For too long have they been left on the back-burner. The gender bias and deep-rooted prejudice and discrimination against the girl child, which have been there down the centuries, are now found to begin in the womb itself. The girl child in the womb faces the peril of pre-birth elimination, i.e. female foeticide. The latest advances in modern medical sciences – tests like amniocentesis and ultrasonography – are being abused. The tests which were originally designed for the detection of gender-related congenital abnormalities in the foetus are now being abused particularly in India and Asian countries, primarily to detect the sex of the foetus with the intention of getting it aborted if it happens to be that of a female. If the female foetus is lucky enough to survive till her birth, then she faces the peril of elimination in infancy through female infanticide. Historically, female infanticide has been in existence since long. Girl infants have been known to be killed by rubbing poison on the mother's breast, by feeding infants with milk of errukam flower or oleander berries, by using sap of calotropis plant, paddy grains, giving sleeping tablets or by simply burying the girl infants alive. Law banned this heinous practice in 1870, more than a century ago. Yet this abuse of girl child, which is a violation of her human right to life, continues to prevail.

The Problem

Female foeticide resulting in decline of child sex ratio has led to enforcement of Pre-conception and Pre-natal Diagnostic Techniques (PNDT) Act since February 2003.

Sex ratio, an important social indicator measuring extent of prevailing equity between males and females in society, is defined as the number of females per 1,000 males. Changes in sex ratio reflect underlying socio-economic and cultural patterns of a society. As per 2001 Census, sex ratio in India is 933 per 1,000 males, which continues to be significantly adverse towards women. Most alarming is decrease in CSR (Child Sex Ratio in age group of 0–6). In Punjab, the number was least (793) in 2001, followed by Haryana (820) and Chandigarh (845). Advances in technology and diagnostic facilities have opened up avenues for the girl haters, leading to serious disturbances in sex ratio as a result of female foeticide. Desire for male child manifests so blatantly that parents have no qualms about repeated, closely-spaced pregnancies, premature deaths and even terminating the child before it is born. Birth of female child is perceived as a curse with economic and social liability.

A 1997 UNFPA report 'India towards Population and Development Goals' estimates that 48 million women are missing from India's population. The report states: 'If the sex ratio of 1,036 females per 1,000 males observed in the state of Kerala in 1991 had prevailed in the whole country, the number of females would be 455 million instead of the 407 million (in the 1991 Census). Thus, there is a case of between 32 and 48 million missing females in the Indian society as of 1991 that needs to be explained.'

This deficit of women has been known to exist even in British India from the time the first census was conducted in 1881 and has only worsened in every subsequent census with the exception in 1981, when it rose in favour of females.

Almost a quarter of India's population consists of girls below 20 years of age. The adolescent girl, who is an embodiment of childhood and womanhood, is barely a shadow in our national policy and is neglected in the fields of health, education and development programmes. Thousands of female infants are murdered in their mother's wombs or are born to die, the justification being that a girl child is better dead in a society which views her as a financial burden. According to UNICEF, 40 to 50 million girls have gone 'missing' in India since 1901 – missing because they were not allowed to be born, or if born, murdered immediately thereafter. Today, India tops the list as far as illegal abortions and female infanticide are concerned. Of the 15 million illegal abortions carried out in the world in 1997, India accounted for four million, 90 per cent of which were intended to eliminate the girl child. While infanticide has a cultural history in India, foeticide is a relatively new phenomenon, permeating societies which had no previous record of infanticide. Aborting of female foetuses has resulted in a skewed sex ratio.

The inhabitants of Punjab, who pioneered the green revolution in the last century, are now heading for a devastating economic and social fallout in the near future due to sharply declining (882 in 1991; 874 in 2001) sex ratio. The reasons of '*son mania*' are socio-cultural, economic and political ones. Among others, the predominant cause is the agrarian set-up associated with the ownership of land and the social infrastructure sustained by Punjabis that accords a low status to women. Chandigarh, the City Beautiful, has the dubious distinction of having the lowest sex ratio (773) in whole of the country despite its high literacy rate of 81.76 per cent. The worst affected districts of Punjab are Ludhiana (824), Fatehgarh Sahib (851) and Patiala (864). This though there has been a 11.4 per cent increase in literacy rate during the last decade (58.5% in 1991; 69.95% in 2001).

'Saheli', a Delhi-based NGO, has reported that during 1978–82, nearly 78,000 female foetuses were aborted after sex determination tests in the country. During 1986–87, 30,000 to 50,000 female foetuses had been aborted. From 1982–92, the number of sex determination clinics multiplied manifold and nearly 13,000 sex determination tests were estimated to have been done in seven Delhi clinics alone. Sex determination techniques began to be publicized through advertisements in newspapers, in trains, buses on walls and pamphlets. Selling the idea of preventing the birth of an unwanted girl child became the order of the day. Though earliest efforts to eradicate female infanticide in India were made in the 19th century during the British rule, the problem of foeticide is a new phenomenon.

Abortion was first legalized under the Indian Penal Code (IPC), which makes the causing of a miscarriage (if not done in good faith to save the life of the woman) an offence punishable with imprisonment up to seven years. Both the doctor and the woman concerned are punishable under this. In case carried out without the consent of the woman (a woman under a misconception, a woman with an unsound mind or in an intoxicated state, and a girl below 12 years of age), the person carrying out such an act is punishable for life. Medical technology makes it easier for parents to discover the sex of a foetus at earlier stages of pregnancy. Such techniques have been developed to check a foetus for genetic or birth disorders, but in societies where son preference is strong, parents are eager to discover the sex of a foetus as soon as possible.

As this technology spreads around the world, many women from communities with a preference for boys practice selective abortion, and abort foetuses solely because they are female. Acting on son preference at an even earlier stage, clinics that offer pre-pregnancy sex-selective technology are doing a booming business despite laws against sex-discriminatory techniques. Coupled with a higher mortality rate for girl children due to neglect or murder, the ratio of women to men has noticeably fallen in India in comparison to countries where female infanticide and selective abortion are not practised. Traditional cultural practices reflect deeply-rooted values and beliefs. Son preference is exhibited in many cultures and is not unique to developing countries or rural areas, although it is stronger in countries where patriarchy and patriliny are prevalent. Societies that expect women to live and express themselves within narrowly defined gender roles also often exhibit cultural practices that benefit men and harm women and girl children. Family lineage and the family name are carried on by male children in many societies, leaving parents concerned about their family's future generations to hope for a son and possibly murder or abort girl children in order to get an heir.

Women who live in societies where they are made miserable through injustice and inequality may not want to raise daughters who will live lives as unhappy as their own. Women have used this excuse as a rationale for killing their girl children. Many women in feudal areas of India do not want to have a daughter who would go through the same misery, humiliation and dependence that seemed to define their own lives. It is difficult to determine how many girl children have been lost to female infanticide and selective abortion. The cultural and economic factors that lead to female infanticide and selective abortion are part of the vicious cycle of discrimination against women and their devaluation. In general, girls still have lower economic earning potential than boys. A poor family may not want the added expense of another child unless that child will someday bring economic wealth back to the family.

As the Indian government increased criminal penalties for female infanticide, the availability of sex-determining technologies such as ultrasound scanning has led to a rise in sex-selective abortion. The Indian Medical Association (IMA) estimates that five million female foetuses are aborted each year, and estimated in 1999 that India had approximately 20,000 ultrasound clinics, most unregistered and staffed by unqualified doctors. In the states of Punjab, Haryana and Uttar Pradesh, mobile vans are used for sex-detection in villages. 'You will find an ultrasound machine even in a village which has a narrow stretch of road where only a bullock cart can go; all that is required is electricity to run the machine and nothing else,' said one ultrasonographist, as reported in *The Hindu*, a national newspaper. The desperation to have a male child by deselecting female child has resulted in the mushrooming growth of sex-determination clinics charging heavy fees, thus making it a profitable business.

Current Scenario

Census 2001 indicates that while there is an increase in the overall sex ratio of the country (927 females per 1,000 males in 1991 to 933 females per 1,000 males in 2001), the child sex ratio (in the 0–6 age group) has shown a decline in almost all the states as compared to the 1991 Census. There are 16 districts in the country having less than 800 girls per 1,000 boys. This means for every 1,000 boys, 200 girls are missing in these districts. Further, there were 70 districts in the country in 2001 where the decline in child sex ratio was more than 50 points when compared with the 1991 Census. Some recent studies conducted to examine the reasons for decline in child sex ratio have also revealed that apart from a strong preference for sons and a low valuation of girls, increasing dowry demands, difficulties involved in bringing up a girl child and an easy availability of ultrasound and abortion services by various private clinics are the main reasons for the increase in female foeticide in the country.

Legal Initiative

To check female foeticide, the Pre-Natal Diagnostic Techniques (Regulation and Prevention of Misuse) Act, 1994 was enacted. The Act came into force in 1996. By itself, it is a comprehensive legislation which lays down the situations in which the use of pre-natal diagnostic techniques is prohibited as also where it is regulated. It has provisions for establishing mechanisms responsible for policy-making under the Act and also those responsible for the implementation of the Act. The penalties for various offences are also elaborated. During the course of the implementation of this Act, certain inadequacies and practical difficulties in its administration came to the Government's notice.

At the same time, newer techniques have been developed to select the sex of the child even before conception, leading to a further decline in the sex ratio. These developments were also taken note of by the Supreme Court in its various orders in a public interest litigation filed by an NGO, CEHAT and Others versus Union of India and Others. The Court had laid down that amendments to the PNDT Act and the amended Act came into force from 14 February 2003. Its main purpose has been to ban the use of sex-selection techniques before or after conception as well as the misuse of pre-natal diagnostic techniques for sex-selective abortions and to regulate such techniques. The implementation of the Act rests with the states and Union Territories.

As a part of the implementation of the Act, appropriate authorities are constituted and each is assisted by an eight-member advisory committee. The committee consists of doctors, lawyers, social workers and officers dealing with the media. Supervisory Boards have also been constituted under the chairpersonship of the Minister of Health and Family Welfare to oversee the implementation of the Act. As per the reports received from states/UTs, more than 21,600 centres conducting pre-natal diagnostic procedure, including ultrasonography, have been registered under the

PC and PNDT Act. So far more than 400 complaints have been filed in various courts for violation of the Act and Rules.

Awareness Campaign

To deal with a problem that has roots in social behaviour and prejudice, mere legislation is not enough. Various activities have been undertaken to create awareness against the practice of pre-natal determination of sex and female foeticide. To implement the provisions of the Act, the help of media units like AIR, Doordarshan, Song and Drama Division, Directorate of Field Publicity, Press Information Bureau, Films Division and DAVP is also being sought. Workshops and seminars have been organized through voluntary organizations at state, regional, district and block levels to create awareness against this social evil. Cooperation has also been sought from religious leaders, as well as the medical fraternity, to curb the practice. A concerted effort involving all sections of the society is necessary to change the prevalent social thinking and remove the gender-based discrimination if the goal of a balanced sex ratio is to be achieved. Keeping this in view, the Government has recently launched a 'Save the Girl Child Campaign'. One of its main objectives is to lessen the preference for a son by highlighting the achievements of young girls.

To achieve the long-term vision, efforts are afloat to create an environment where sons and daughters are equally valued. Such efforts cannot take place in isolation or in relation to a single issue of female foeticide. They have to be integrated into the larger advocacy and communication efforts that are already taking place. Legislation and regulation provide a framework within which the role of multiple actors and institutions can be concretely measured and evaluated. A number of measures can be taken to ensure effective implementation. For example, under both the MTP Act, 1971 and the PNDT Act, 1994, specific sites have been classified for legal provision of these services. Universal registration of these sites and listing of diagnostic equipment, granting licences and requiring that they be prominently displayed, among others, could help curb misuse. The PNDT Act can be the first step in a broader effort to regulate the private health care sector.

Eradication of Sex-Related Harmful Practices

Related to the problem of gender bias and the persistent discrimination against the girl child are the sex-related harmful practices of female foeticide and female infanticide, leading to the most unwanted abortions and the present high rates of female infant mortality of 70.8 (1999), female child mortality of 24.5 (1997) and maternal mortality of 407 (1998). Based on the 1991 Census, 65 districts have been identified as problem districts, with sex ratio abnormally in favour of males between 1,100 and 1,218 males for 1,000 females in the states of Andhra Pradesh, Bihar, Delhi, Gujarat, Haryana, Madhya Pradesh, Punjab, Rajasthan, Tamil Nadu and Uttar Pradesh.

Besides, a multi-centric study sponsored by the Department of Women and Child Development in 1993 also confirmed that while female foeticide is being practised all over the country, female infanticide exists as a local phenomenon amongst certain communities. The Tenth Plan has initiated action to enforce effectively both the Indian Penal Code, and the Pre-Natal Diagnostic Technique (Regulation and Prevention of Misuse) Act, 1994 to control/eradicate female foeticide and female infanticide, respectively, with a very close vigil and surveillance along with severe punishment for the guilty. Along with this, long-term measures of sensitizing the society to change their mind-set, which is negatively disposed towards the girl child as unwanted, neglected and discriminated both within and outside her home, will also be put into action throughout the country with a special focus on the problem districts and problem communities.

Strategy for Elimination of Female Foeticide

It is not poverty alone that makes families kill their children. The community too acts in strange ways to perpetuate the crime by ridiculing couples who do not have a male child. Illiteracy, ignorance of the welfare scheme available for the girl child and poverty alleviation, the legal implication of indulging in female infanticide, the dowry system are some of the reasons for failure of the schemes and interventions undertaken by the government and NGOs to eradicate female infanticide. The long-term strategies should include education and empowerment of women. Empowerment of rural marginalized women and education to improve their lot will heighten their status in the society.

As the women groups and the federation gain in importance and play a greater role in the development of the area, it is hoped that their presence and the politico-economic strength they enable will help curb the practice. Media, both print and electronic, can play a very significant role in removing gender bias and developing a positive image of the girl child in the society, but in a county like ours where there are problems in reaching the backward rural and tribal areas, a mix of mass media with various traditional forms of communication may provide a more effective alternative to influence the illiterate and the poor. Enhancing sensitization to gender issues to influence the policy-makers, planners, administrators and enforcement machinery is another important strategy.

The Nodal Department of Women and Child Development has launched special efforts to develop a positive image of the girl child and women. It is not easy to change overnight the attitude of even women towards female infanticide. Even if the women are prepared to understand and accept the need to change, the social situation and the family environment prevent them from doing so. Therefore, young married couples and pregnant women are given counseling so that they could cope with the situation, because they are surrounded by in-laws and neighbours who are pro-female infanticide.

The practice of using amniocentesis for sex determination is banned through law and practitioners indulging in or abetting such acts should be punished severely. Amniocentesis, where necessary, will be performed only in government or approved medical institutions to prevent the practice of using amniocentesis for purpose of sex determination. Public education on the illegality of foetal sex determination and sex-selection abortion should be accompanied by positive messages on the value of daughters. Advertising of sex-determination techniques shall be banned forthwith and stringent measures will be taken against the offenders.

Media will be effectively used to bring about attitudinal changes towards the girl child. Priority will be given to educating parents on the importance of providing adequate food for the girl child. Extensive use of media for the sensitive promotion of a positive image of women and girls should be looked into. Development of school-based strategies for inculcating of positive self-image amongst girls should be encouraged. Concerted efforts to break the gender stereotypes particularly at the +2 level and conscious inputs into curriculum, textbooks, teacher education, institutional planning supported by career guidance, counseling should be given importance. Special awareness generation programmes and campaigns to sensitize the public should be highlighted. For keeping a close watch on the pregnant women for six months (three months before delivery and three months after it), panchayat-level vigilance committees should be formed. Female infanticide programmes should include strategies to modify and liberalize the traditional cultural values that are strongly held by the affected communities.

For such programmes to be effective, it must cultivate in the affected communities more positive attitudes and acceptance of social change, particularly in relation to girl children. Such intervention programmes should target middle socio-economic groups in which the tendency and probability of female infanticide is supposed to be higher. Also, these programmes should target the male population of the affected communities, since compared to females, males are more vulnerable to developing a tendency toward female infanticide. Since the probability of female infanticide is indicated in many of the affected communities, NGOs working in these areas must build up legal and social pressure to counter this practice. Intervention programmes for mid-wives must be implemented.

The Pre-Natal Diagnostic Techniques (Regulation and Prevention of Misuse) Act, was enacted on 28 September 1994, which banned sex determination tests all over the country. This Act carries a three-year imprisonment sentence and a ₹ 10,000 fine for offenders. The implementation of this Act initially faced problems as monitoring agencies had to be identified at all levels. It was therefore only in 1997 when the responsibility was delegated that actual implementation of the Act began. Despite this, there is still a social complacency among all sections of society, which needs to be corrected at the earliest. A great deal of attention is being paid to the status and well-being of the girl child by the government, UN agencies, NGOs and welfare organizations. Since the law against sex determination was passed, most people feel their conscience has been assuaged. But the problem has gone underground. Media attention has been flimsy, reporting a few instances with no serious focus on the issue.

Possible Hazards

It has been seen that populations with more number of males remain at risk of social unrest with an increase in crime and violence against women like dowry death, child marriage, bride selling, kidnapping, rape, etc. The risk of polyandry also exists in such a society. Stringent measures need to be taken to end this discriminating offence. Education system should promote gender equality right from school. Family with strong male bias should be psychologically counseled. So far as sex selection as an offence is concerned, it should be made cognizable and tried under the same section as attempt to murder (Section 307 of IPC). Also, setting up self-help groups among women, targeting educated women, rewarding all-girl families, setting up helplines, adopting new social customs, banning dowry stringently, registering and taking care of expectant mothers, including postpartum follow-up, rewarding voluntary sterilization in girl-dominating families, etc., are some other measures.

Conclusion and Suggestive Measures

Instead of decennial surveys, annual appraisal of sex ratio in the worst-affected states and districts should be done. Daughters should get the right to perform the last rites of their parents equivalent to that of sons. The government should amend the existing laws of inheritance. The daughter should be accepted as heir to ancestral property legally as well as socially. Exemplary punishment should be given to the doctors who aid or indulge in this heinous practice of conducting sex determination tests. Such doctors should be punished by MCI under the offence of professional misconduct. We should not wait for social transformation to take care of this burning issue. We may be paving way for more hazardous technologies that may have more catastrophic results. There is an urgent need to change the mindset of people. The Millennium Development Goals of gender equality and the empowerment of common man should be on top priority. India's missing women cannot be brought back to life but the future generations of women can be protected if we take the campaign against female feticide on a war footing.

The following suggestive measures are recommended:

- Laws have been passed declaring female foeticide as illegal. Advertising for pre-natal prediction of sex has also been declared illegal. Efforts should be made to implement these laws effectively. Strict punishment should be given to the defaulters.
- The trend of taking and giving of dowry, which takes place mostly in educated and upper class homes, cannot be discouraged by laws alone. Efforts should continue to be made at the individual as well as at the government

level. Stringent and effective laws should be supported by speedy trials, dowry giving and taking cases should be tried by a special court and short stay homes should be set up for battered women.

- Efforts and provisions should be made to provide social security to parents who are above 65 years of age and have only daughters. They should be provided with old-age pension if they do not have a son. Most of the respondents in the study who had daughters feared for their social security, especially in old age.
- Girl children should be provided free and compulsory education up to higher secondary level. This would decrease the so-called unnecessary investment on girl children made by the parents on their daughters. They would stop taking their daughters as a liability.
- Certain schemes should be started for providing economic provisions for the female children. For this purpose, government should start various employment schemes for females where 100 per cent reservation could be made for women in occupations like teaching, nursing, telephone operators, etc.
- Women's right to own and inherit property and the social obligation of daughters to support parents in the same way as sons, can be spread by policy intervention to inculcate these new values in households as well as legal support to implement these values should be provided.
- Religious education can play a role by preaching against female foeticide, dowry and discrimination against the girl children. Moral education should be imparted in schools. Children should be taught to uphold morals and refrain from practices of dowry, female foeticide and gender bias. The vulnerable minds of the children should be so influenced that they grow up as adults who consider practising dowry and female foeticide as immoral.
- Various monetary benefits should be provided to parents having daughters. Only the state of Tamil Nadu has offered a savings bond of ₹ 2,000 to families that

accept sterilization after bearing two daughters and no son. It has also started a scheme whereby girls from Scheduled Castes after completing grade VIII could receive a bonus of ₹ 5,000.

- Women should also be socialized from early childhood to consider themselves as equal to men. They should be encouraged to assume all those responsibilities which are normally considered to be belonging to the male domain. This would be a positive influence on the coming generations as today's girl child would be tomorrow's mother as well as mother in-law.

Last, but not the least, everyone should imbibe the divine revelation received by Guru Nanak and preached to all his followers: '*From woman man is born; within woman man is conceived; to woman he is engaged and married; woman becomes his friend; when his woman dies, he seeks another woman; to woman he is bound. So why call her bad? From her kings are born.*'

References

Bandewar, S. 2003. 'Abortion Services and Providers' Perceptions: Gender Dimensions', *Economic and Political Weekly*, Vol. XXXVIII, No. 21, 24–30 May, pp. 2075–81.

Census of India. 2001.

Desai, N. 1988. 'Born to Die', *The Indian Post*, Bombay, 7 October.

Diaz, A.A. 1988. 'Amniocentesis and Female Foeticide', *Bulletin of the Indian Federation of Medical Guild*, July.

Giriraj, R. 2004. 'Changing Attitude to Female Infanticide in Salem', *Journal of Social Welfare*, Vol. 50, No. 11, February, pp. 13–14 and 34–35.

Kollor, T.M. 1990. 'Female Infanticide: A Psychological Analysis', *Grass Roots Action: Special Issue on Girl Child*, 3 April, p. 3.

Krishna Kumar, A. 1992. 'Female Infanticide Beyond Symptoms: Will the Government Measures Help?', *Frontline*, 4 December.

Kumari, R. 1995. 'Rural Female Adolescence: Indian Scenario', *Social Change*, Vol. 25, No. 2, pp. 177–88.

Mallick, A. 2004. 'India's Missing Women', *Social Welfare*, July, pp. 4–10.

Mane, P.N. 1991. 'Socialization of Hindu Women in Their Childhood: An Analysis of Literature', *The Journal of Family Welfare*, Vol. 52, No. 1, pp. 81–96.

Patel, V. 1994. 'Indian Women's Struggle to Survive: Campaign Against Femicide', in UNICEF, *The Child and the Law*, New Delhi, pp. 60–61.

Puri, N. 1998. 'The Girl Child in India', *The Journal of Family Welfare*, Vol. 44, No. 3, pp. 1–8.

Rao, R. 2004. 'Missing Girls of Punjab', *Social Welfare*, March, pp. 37–38.

Srivastava, R.D. 2000. 'Girls are Second-class Citizens Everywhere', *The Times of India*, 17 January, p. 3.

Yadav, S. and V.S. Badari. 1999. 'Gender Preference and Anxiety of Pregnant Women', *The Indian Journal of Social Work*, Vol. 60, No. 4, pp. 538–51.

7

Behavioural Categorization of Women Based on Empowerment Level and the Extent of Son-Preference

A Case Study of Patna

Dweepika Kumari

Indian women are generally considered to be quite traditional having a strong son/male preference and belief in the established patriarchal setup of the society and further, they also tend to impart these traditional values to their daughters and daughters-in-law. The young women, who are thus conditioned from their very childhood, tend to be meek and docile, lose their self-confidence and always silently submit to whatever is imposed on them. Though the increasing level of education has increased their level of confidence and made their views independent, they still remain socially conditioned and often compromise their own ideologies just to satisfy their family.

But now, there are quite a significant number of women who are not only confident of themselves and free of traditional bindings on their mentality but also vehemently oppose female foeticide and support the assertion of women's rights. The increasing level of education and emancipation, however, does not always create a positive mindset among the women.

There are many who, in this age of commercialization, tend to become money-minded and do not hesitate from committing foeticide citing the traditional reasons as an excuse. Thus, the women have a diverse nature considering their extent of son-preference and their empowerment level.

Research Problem

The research problem taken up for the present study was that not all the women have the same attitude towards the prevailing socio-economic phenomena of son-preference and daughter-discrimination and thus, diverse methods are necessary to combat the menace of declining sex ratio.

Objectives

The present paper is an attempt to show that the women in our society are of a diverse mindset and have varying son-preferring and daughter-discriminating attitudes and thus, hold varying perceptions towards the much talked challenge about the declining sex ratio.

The study was taken up with the following objectives in mind:

- To develop a method for the behavioural categorization of women depending upon their attitude towards son-preference and their level of empowerment.
- To suggest diverse strategies to combat the declining sex ratio according to different behavioural categories.

Study Area

The capital city of Bihar, Patna has been selected as the study area for the present research work. Patna is the second largest city in eastern India. It has been selected as a study area for this research as it provides a great variety in the nature of the respondents. It being the capital city attracts migrants from all parts of the state and even from other neighbouring states. The women who often migrate with their spouses, thus, belong to various religions, castes and economic background. The respondents are not only city-bred but also women from rural background.

Methodology of Behavioural Categorization of Women

The present paper is entirely based on the empirical observations of the author supported by the data collected during a primary level random sample survey using a questionnaire. The survey covers 1,040 women across the study area.

For the behavioural categorization of women, four main parameters were taken which were further sub-divided into seven. They are:

• Empowerment level	• Mobility autonomy • Decision-making autonomy
• Son-Preference	• Inclination towards son • Reason for son-preference
• Daughter-discrimination	• Justification of female feticide • Reason for justification of female feticide
• Assertiveness towards rights	• Views towards reporting of domestic violence
• Measuring the empowerment level	

Mobility Autonomy

Freedom of mobility is an important indicator of the autonomy of women. The ease, confidence and the freedom with which a woman can go to various places like local markets, neighbours, hospitals and friends and relatives within the city or outside it, reflects her mobility.

In this section, the author has attempted to develop a proper methodology to assess the level of freedom the women enjoy regarding their mobility. The mobility index sums up the weightage given to movement of females visiting four different categories of locations – local market, hospital, friends and relatives within the town and lastly, outside the town to which a woman can go unescorted. Again, the intention was to select a range of places both within the city and outside it, both easy and difficult to access.

For this purpose, the author has given proportionate weightage to different parameters because the author realizes that all the variables cannot be given equal weightage. The values allotted to different parameters are subjective, depending on the author's own perception and conclusion drawn on the basis of the responses gathered during the field survey as expressed by women respondents.

The weightage accorded for different places, which depends basically upon the unescorted and free movement of a woman as also upon the ease or difficulty of access, is as follows:

Table 1

Weightage Accorded to Mobility of Women in Different Conditions

Place	*Alone*	*Escorted*	*Rarely/ Never at all*
Market	4	2	1
Hospital	5	3	1
Friends and relatives within city	5	2	1
Outside city	6	3	1

Method: The proportionate weightage method.

Explanation of the weightage accorded to the mobility of women.

Mobility to the market: Going to the local market, especially for regular household shopping for vegetables, groceries, etc. is a necessity for most of the housewives who are controlling the household expenditure budget. Since this is a very common and regular feature for the women, only 4 points are given for going out unescorted. But if they need to be compulsorily escorted while going to the market also, then this indicates restricted mobility; hence, here only 2 points have been given. In some cases the women are not at all allowed to go to these places even with an escort, which reflects extraordinary restrictions on women's movement; hence, only 1 point is given.

Mobility to the hospitals: In case of visit to the hospitals, which generally is not a common need or regular phenomena, but sometimes becomes of utmost importance. So, if the respondent never goes even to the hospital alone in spite of urgent need, then this indicates the denial of her minimal needs of health care along with the restricted mobility. As such, in this case, they are given the lowest weightage, i.e. since visit to a hospital is often only in case of being ill or while accompanying some ill family member, e.g. son, daughter, brother, mother, father, in-laws, etc., having an escort proves to be helpful. Therefore, going with an escort may not necessarily mean lack of freedom. Hence, in this case, 3 points have been given. However, if at times of need a woman is able to go to such a place alone, then this reflects her boldness, confidence, decision-making capability and freedom. So here, she is accorded 5 points. Also, easy access to hospitals provides them awareness about reproductive health care and family planning methods; this also boosts their reproductive autonomy.

Mobility within the city: In case of visiting friends and relatives within the city, it is an optional or choice-related decision, i.e. if the women are easily moving within the city for visiting their friends and relatives unescorted, this clearly reflects a higher degree of freedom of mobility being enjoyed by the women. Here, it should also be noted that contact with friends and relatives gives a boost to their decision-making autonomy, as such they are given 5 points. Now since this movement is within the city which is quite accessible, the respondents are given only 2 points if they have to be necessarily accompanied by someone else, especially males. Only 1 point is given if they are rarely allowed to go, which not only restricts their mobility but also their interaction with their friends and close relatives.

Mobility outside the city: In this last case, i.e. the movement outside the city is not a very common or regular feature for the women. Even if they have to go to their relatives or for tours, it is generally along with their whole families or accompanied with senior/adults, especially male members. The security factor or the inconvenience factor for women in trains or new places deters people from allowing their womenfolk or even the women themselves from moving out alone. In many cases, women themselves feel insecure and less confident to handle the situation of travelling alone; therefore, in spite of no restrictions being imposed, they preferably opt to travel with their male family members, e.g. father, husband or son. Therefore, moving outside the town with an escort is rated as 3 points on the mobility index. Only the most confident and bold ones venture outside the town unescorted. This reflects the highest degree of freedom of mobility and thus, is accorded 6 points on the mobility index.

Next, the individual weightage points have been summed up to find the mobility index. Following is an example of the emerging result.

Table 2

Mobility of Women

S.No.	*Local Market*	*Hospital*	*Within City*	*Outside City*	*Mobility Index*
1.	4	3	2	3	12
2.	4	5	5	6	20
3.	2	3	2	3	10
4.	1	1	1	1	4
5.	4	3	5	3	15
6.	4	3	2	1	10
7.	2	3	1	1	7

Mobility Index

The mobility index is thus, calculated on the basis of the different weightage given to the different variables. The highest weightage accorded to any respondent in the case where she was able to move about everywhere unescorted is 20 and the lowest weightage was 4 (when she rarely or never moves out of her house in any case). Thus, the mobility index ranges from 4 to 20. The level of freedom of mobility of each respondent was fixed according to this mobility index.

Table 3

Mobility Index

Sum of Weightage Points	*Mobility Level*
4–8	Very Low
9–11	Low
12–16	Moderate
17–20	High

Decision-Making Autonomy

The Indian culture is 'largely gender-stratified, characterized by patrilineal descent, patrilocal residence, inheritance and succession practices that exclude women and hierarchical relations in which the patriarch has authority over the family members. Tight control is exerted over the women in every sphere of their lives – their free movement, their voice in family affairs, their economic independence and their relations with their husbands' (Jejeebhoy and Sathar, 2001). Women have comparatively no or very little decision-making (DM) autonomy and authority in such a societal setup.

However, the level and pattern of women's DM autonomy varies considerably from region to region. There is also much variation in female autonomy among different religious groups, castes, age groups and economic classes. Level of autonomy is also greatly affected by their position in family, their educational level and employment status.

In this context, a DM Index has developed which reflects the level of autonomy of the respondents surveyed. This DM Index is the sum of weightage (or points) accorded to the women on different aspects depending upon their level of participation in decision-making. This is reflected by the main decision-making authority in different aspects.

Method for Calculation of Decision-Making Index

A strategy of subjective proportionate weightage technique has been adopted here according to the significance level perceived by the scholar herself during the survey, keeping in view the social system and the prevailing norms. Proportionate weightage has been given to the individual aspect depending upon their importance level. The aspects which have greater impact on the autonomy of women, e.g. the number and timing of children or her mobility have been given higher weightage while general or day-to-day matters like cooking of food, etc., which have less significance, have been given lesser weightage.

Table 4

Weightage on Different Decision-Making Parameters

Matters of Decision	*Self*	*Husband*	*Both*	*Others*
No. and timing of children	6	3	4	1
Visit to friends/relatives	6	3	4	2
Major household purchases	5	2	4	3
Cooking food	4	1	3	2

Number and Timing of Children

As this comes under the reproductive rights, this is one of the few decisions of which a woman should have total control. As this decision gives a woman control over her own body, this aspect is of paramount importance, so it has been given the highest weightage, i.e. 6 points. This decision if taken in mutual understanding with the husband, which is the common case, also reflects cordial mutual relationship and thus is given 4 points. In some cases a woman also accepts her husband's wishes even if she does not desire the same, simply to please him or maintain their cordial relation. Thus, in such cases, 3 points are given. However, when this decision is influenced by others (in-laws), i.e. when she is forced to undergo several pregnancies against her wishes, she loses all her reproductive rights and so only 1 point is given.

Visit to Friends and Relatives

This decision relates to the personal freedom of a woman, i.e. freedom of mobility. This freedom of mobility allows a woman to come out of the confines of the four walls of her house into the contact with the outer world, broadens her mental horizons and gives her confidence. As this aspect also deals with the contact with her friends and natal kin which boosts her autonomy, the self decision-making rights of a woman and thus is given 6 points. Mutual decision of husband and wife in this regard is granted 4 points. This decision when taken by others, i.e. mother-in-law, father-in-law, etc., though indicates restriction on a woman's freedom but this is also a reflection of our cultural tradition where the elders' permission is considered necessary and thus is given 2 points.

Major Household Purchases

Purchasing of household items is a matter of household issues. Having control over these decisions reflects a greater say in the household affairs and thus economic decision-making autonomy. Mutual decision-making in this regard is given 4 points. In case this decision is taken by others, i.e. the in-laws, this reflects that the elders in the family are in control of financial matters and that the woman at a later age has a greater chance of gaining more economic autonomy and thus is given 3 points. The husband being the sole decision-maker in this regard indicates total lack of participation by women and is given 2 points.

Food to be Cooked

The kitchen from time immemorial has been considered as the traditional arena of women and cooking as the sole responsibility of women, therefore decision regarding this has been left entirely to them. Thus, this is not a significant indicator of the autonomy of women and hence the woman has been given 4 points if she is the sole decision-maker in this regard, and 3 points in case of mutual decisions. Sometimes she also cooks according to the wishes of the family members; consequently, 2 points are given in this condition. However, if the food is cooked solely according to the husband's wish or choice with her negligible participation, she is given only 1 point.

Later, the individual weightage points have been summed up to find out the Decision-Making Index (DM Index). The result comes out in the following way.

S. No.	*Household Purchases*	*Cooking Food*	*Visiting Friends*	*No. and Timing of Children*	*DM Index*
1	5	4	6	6	21
2	5	4	6	4	19
3	5	4	4	4	17
4	3	3	2	4	12
5	2	1	3	1	7
6	4	3	4	4	15
7	3	4	4	3	14

Decision-Making Index

The decision-making index (DM Index) is, thus, calculated on the basis of the different weightage given to the different variables. The highest weightage accorded to any respondent in the case where she was able to take the decision on her own ranges from 4 to 6 depending upon the relative importance of that variable and the lowest weightage was 1 to 3. Thus, the decision-making index ranges from 7 to 21. The level of decision-making autonomy of each respondent was fixed according to decision-making index.

Table 5

Decision-Making Index

Sum of Decision-Making Weightage Points	*Autonomy Level*
7–12	Very less
13–15	Less
16–18	Moderate
19–21	High

Assessing the Son-Preference

Son-preference in India is a well-documented phenomenon and its implications on skewed sex ratio and female feticide have not drawn enough attention of policy-makers till now. The term 'son-preference' refers to the attitude that sons are more important and more valuable than the daughters ... Parents prize their sons for economic, religious and social reasons.

Indian women in general are characterized by a strong son-preference. In a rigid patrilineal society, a woman attains and commands dignity and respect in the family mainly when she gives birth to a son and the sons becoming a lifetime protection against insecurity results in a strong urge among the females to have a son.

This urge to have a son is so strong that even the first-born girl child is not so welcomed in the family. Having a son as the first issue satiates them and only then they are prepared to accept the next child as daughters. Even then, the percentage of women who want more sons than daughters is quite high especially in North India.

Inclination Towards Son

A set of questions was asked to assess the inclination of women towards sons. The questions were:

- What would you prefer as your first child?
- If the first two consecutive children are of same sex (either male or female), what would they do:
  - Stop
  - Make one more attempt
  - Abort

Reason for Son-Preference

As the next step, the women who exhibited son-preference were asked to state the most important reason for preferring a son from among the following listed reasons. The answers stated by them helped to analyse the factors which motivate, convince, prompt or compel a woman towards son-preference.

Q. You would prefer a son because:

- Problem of dowry for girls
- Sons carry family name
- To perform the last rites
- To give financial support in old age
- To provide protection in old age
- Not having sons causes family rejection
- Having sons gives social prestige
- Daughters do not stay along after marriage
- Problem of security for girls

(Questions asked in the questionnaire)

Analysing Daughter-Discrimination

The worst form of daughter-discrimination in India is manifested in the form of female foeticide. Female foeticide refers to the sex-selective abortion of the female child. In India, this practice has started showing its deeply negative impact in the form of an alarmingly low sex ratio, particularly child sex ratio (only 914 females per 1,000 males in 2011).

The cultural preferences for sons rather than daughters have resulted in skewed sex ratios in India. The menace of female foeticide started emerging and spreading all over northern and western India and later on all over the country. 'Today, female foeticide is no more an urban phenomenon, rural people are also getting more and more involved in it and come all the way long to cities to get these tests done' (Savanoor, 2009).

Whether Female Foeticide is Justified or Not?

The practice of female foeticide on such a large scale also makes one point clear that there are many who justify and accept this act. Although while in open most of the people seem to oppose female foeticide citing it to be a cruel practice, yet behind closed doors, it is still a widely practised method of attaining the desired gender composition of one's progeny. Though most of the women do agree that this act is neither morally or legally right, many of them do give some justifications for this heinous crime. Surprisingly, some of these women seem to willingly accept and even support this barbaric practice citing socio-economic reasons.

This attitude is a further parameter adopted for the behavioural categorization of women.

- Whether female foeticide is justified or not?
- What is the reason for justification of female foeticide?

For the second question, the following several options were given:

- If the couple already has two daughters and now wants a son
- If the parents are financially weak
- If there is pressure from the in-laws to go in for an abortion
- If the husband desires a son and is pressuring for abortion
- Any other reason

The two questions together reveal whether they are justifying female foeticide willingly or under pressure or compulsion and if willingly, then what is the motivating factor – tradition or money?

Assertiveness Towards Rights

Today's women have enough strength and boldness to oppose any act of infringement upon their basic human rights, i.e. right over their own body and right to live without any fear. Domestic violence whether physical, mental or emotional is a violation of a woman's right to live without fear while pressuring a woman to undergo multiple abortions in the quest of a son is a violation of a woman's reproductive rights. Women empowerment should also include her ability to oppose any kind of such violations of her rights.

The last parameter taken here was whether any incident of forced female foeticide (i.e. against the wishes of women) or violence for this purpose should be reported to the police or any women's organization or not so that some action could be taken against the guilty. The question had to be answered by choosing one of the following three options, i.e. Yes, No

Table 6

Criteria for Categorization of Women

Category	*Mobility Autonomy*	*Decision-Making Autonomy*	*Son-Preference*	*Son-Preference Reason*	*Is Female Foeticide Justified?*	*Foeticide Justification Reason?*	*Reporting of Domestic Violence*
Traditional	Low/Moderate/High	Less/Moderate/High	Yes	For family heir/funeral rites/protection and support/social prestige/girl's security	Yes	Too many daughters/pressure of husband or in-laws	No/No use
Traditional but no female foeticide	Low/Moderate/High	Less/Moderate/High	Yes	For family heir/funeral rites/protection and support/social prestige/girl's security	No	–	No/No use/Yes
Traditional but economically motivated	Low/Moderate/High	Less/Moderate/High	Yes	Dowry problem	Yes	Too many daughters/poverty	No/No use/Yes
Submissive	V. Low/Low/Moderate/High	V. Less/Less/Moderate	Yes	For family heir/funeral rites/fear of rejection by family/social prestige	Yes	Pressure of husband or in-laws	No/No use/Yes
Compromising	Low/Moderate/High	Less/Moderate/High	No	–	Yes	Pressure of husband or in-laws	No/No use/Yes
Independent (views)	Low/Moderate	Less/Moderate	No	–	No	–	No/No use
Independent and bold	Moderate/High	Less/Moderate/High	No	–	No	–	Yes

and No Use. This question was an attempt to study the level of assertiveness of women.

Behavioural Categories of Women

Depending upon the level of son-preference, the respondents can be grouped into distinct categories. This categorization of women takes into account their son-preferring attitude and the reason for son-preference, their reason for justification of female foeticide and their attitude towards domestic violence. The factors which influence their attitude, i.e. basically their autonomy level regarding their decision-making and mobility, have also been taken into account while formulating this categorization.

On the basis of the above criteria, the women can be grouped into seven broad categories:

- Traditional son-preferring women justifying female foeticide (Trad.)
- Traditional son-preferring women but not justifying female foeticide (Trad. Nff.)
- Traditional but economically motivated (Trad. Eco.)
- Submissive women
- Compromising women
- Women having independent views but reluctant to take a action (Ind. views)
- Women having independent views and bold enough to take their own stand (Ind. Bold)

Traditional Son-Preferring Women

These are those women who are traditionally and socially conditioned into having a strong son-preference. Mostly the reason stated by them for having a strong son-preference is either a son being very necessary for continuance of the family name or for performing the last funeral rites of their parents without which a person does not get '*moksha*'.

The concept of a girl child being a 'paraya dhan' is also quite common among such women. They state that after their marriage the girls have to go to their husband's home and they would remain all alone if they have only daughters. As such, sons become necessary to give them company. As the daughters do not remain with their parents, the sons become all the more important to provide them financial support and protection in old age. Such women also consider their male progeny as a source of strength.

Mostly such women justify female foeticide if the couple already has two or three daughters. Because nowadays, people do not prefer having many children and sons being most desired to carry their family's name, they consider it better to abort the unborn female child.

Though they enjoy moderate to high mobility and decision-making autonomy, they also accept domestic violence as though it is natural and social phenomena and do not prefer reporting such matters saying that finally a woman has to live with her husband and in-laws only. Out of the total women surveyed, 25 per cent (259) women fall in this category, i.e. one-fourth of the total respondents covered under the survey come in this category.

Traditional but Do not Prefer Female Foeticide

The women of this category are similar to the traditional women in all respects except that they do not support female foeticide. Though they too consider sons to be very important but feel that aborting a female foetus is gruesome and similar to murder and therefore a sin. About 6 per cent of the surveyed women (61) come in this category. Many of them also suggested adopting a son if the couple does not beget a son.

Traditional but Mostly Economically Motivated

The reason for the son-preference for some women is not traditional/cultural in any sense, i.e. for continuation of family name or for performing funeral rites; rather, it is purely for economic motive. Their main reason for son-preference is that marriages in our system are based on dowry, i.e. exorbitant dowry has to be paid for the marriage of their daughters. They lament that after meeting all the general requirements like education, clothing, etc., of their daughters, they cannot afford to pay the heavy demands of dowry so it becomes necessary to keep the number of girl children in limits. For this, they are also ready for aborting their female foetus. About 5 per cent (56) women come in this category, many of whom have already undergone such an operation.

Submissive Women

As the name suggests, the women of this category are those whose own thinking and views are highly subdued by those of her husband and/or in-laws and affected by societal pressure. As remarked by a respondent, 'Often after a girl gets married, she covers her independent spirit with a blanket of the views of her in-laws and her actions are guided by their wishes', i.e. the decisions, actions and her movements are all determined by the whims and wishes of her husband and his family.

About 9 per cent (92) women belong to this category. Such women or girls have been traditionally and socially conditioned by their families to accept each and every wish and order of her in-laws by saying that the dignity and the honour of her family depends on her actions and full obedience to her in-laws. Thus, they are conditioned to accept every demand of in-laws in the name of family honour. As a result, they have no opinion of their own. Their reason for son-preference is either traditional (for a family heir or for performance of last rites) or compulsion, i.e. fear of family rejection or ill-treatment or societal pressure in form of tantrums from the relatives or neighbours.

Often such women are economically dependent and too meek to offer any resistance and as such justify female foeticide done under compulsion of husband or in-laws.

A long period of subjugation suppresses any confidence or courage to oppose any ill-treatment meted out to them and they simply accept domestic violence as a part and parcel of life. When asked whether such incidents of domestic violence should be reported or not, a majority of such women either said 'No' (due to fear of desertion by the marital family) or 'No use' (due to hassling legal processes or traditional customs). Only a few of them replied to this question in affirmation.

Compromising Women

These are those women who have independent thinking or views that are not bound by traditional or societal prejudiced views against the girl child. Such women do not differentiate between sons and daughters but they too have been socially conditioned to accept the views of in-laws. They just compromise with their own views and ideologies just to satisfy in-laws and keep the family intact.

A significant number of women, i.e. 30 (29%) are of this nature. Often many of these women also state that even the pressure of in-laws for undergoing female foeticide does not matter at all. Even the husband has to be tried to be convinced but in case he does not, the woman has to undergo an abortion of the female foetus. Many of these women who justified female foeticide on this account said that even under pressure this should be done only once and not more than that. This becomes necessary to save her family as it is her husband with whom she has to spend her whole life.

Thus, the difference between submissive and compromising women is only that while the former offer no resistance and meekly accept any unreasonable demand of her husband and/or in-laws (abortion of female foetus in this case), the latter accepts it only as a last resort after making attempts to make them change their mind. Differentiation between submissive and compromising women is also based on the fact that while submissive women have a lower confidence level and have only low to moderate autonomy, the compromising women have a comparatively higher level of confidence and enjoy a moderate to high level of autonomy.

Independent but Only in Views

These are those women who are free from the gender-bias mindset and denounce female foeticide. However, they do not strongly assert their autonomy, i.e. do not actively participate in the decision-making process. They mostly have low to moderate autonomy. Also when asked whether the incidents of domestic violence or forcing women to undergo abortion should be reported or not, they answered either in negative or that it is of no use, i.e. though they oppose female foeticide under all conditions, they lack the strength or courage to report any action of domestic violence. About 11 per cent of surveyed women (115) come in this category.

Independent and Bold

These are the progressive women who are independent of any orthodox thinking, neither they are submissive to the whims of their husband or in-laws nor do they compromise in face of opposition to their decision. They believe in the equality of the sexes and that both sons and daughters should be given equal rights and treatment. They strongly condemn gender discrimination and the inhumane practice of female foeticide. These are those women who are bold enough to assert their views and have their say accepted. They enjoy moderate to high level of autonomy and have a greater say in their family matters. They not only strongly oppose female foeticide but also support reporting any incidences of domestic violence. They are strong-willed, full of confidence, having a modern outlook towards life and advocate gender equality in the society. About 15 per cent of the women (152) covered under the present survey can be said to be bold and independent.

Result of the Sample Survey Conducted in the Study Area

Table 7

Behavioural Categorization of Women in Patna

Category of Women	*Total*	*In %*
Traditional	259	25
Traditional but no female foeticide	61	6
Traditional but economically motivated	56	5
Submissive	92	9
Compromising	301	29
Independent (Only in views)	115	11
Independent and bold	152	15

Conclusion

The study suggests that women are quite varied in nature when it comes to their son-preference and daughter-discriminating nature. There are various factors which cause these variations, like their upbringing (traditional or liberal), education, financial dependence/independence, etc.

The purpose of this study was to highlight the fact that different women have different reasons for preferring sons and shying away from daughters. Thus, the policy-makers should be clear that like for different diseases we require different medicines, similarly to treat the problem of son-preference/daughter-discrimination, a different approach is necessary for each different category of women stated here to steer them away from son-preference and/or daughter-discrimination. For example:

- Traditional son-preferring women – Promoting anti-female foeticide campaign by religious leaders might prove to be fruitful.
- Traditional son-preferring women but not supporting female foeticide – Promoting and highlighting the rising gender equality through ad-campaigns, anti-dowry campaigns and giving boost to girl education and female employment is an effective method to nullify the negative mindset of girl as a burden.
- Traditional economic-minded women – Stringent anti-dowry laws and providing monetary incentives for girl-education.
- Submissive – Promoting empowerment of women through education and employment
- Compromising
  - In case of financial compulsions – Providing economic independence through job incentives.
  - In case of social compulsions to save one's family (pressure of marital family) – Initiating an 'anti-female foeticide campaign' to create a social environment

which looks down upon the people promoting female foeticide and supports women fighting for the assertion of their rights might prove to be a good idea.

- Independent but only in views – Setting up of NGOs supporting women issues and making the legal procedures less cumbersome and more women-friendly.

Thus, the author concludes that there is a strong need to bring about diversity in the approaches towards the method to check the rapidly declining sex ratio, keeping in mind the different behavioural attitude of women towards son-preference/daughter-discrimination.

References

Bisaria, Akhilesh. 2007. 'Female Foeticide: Socio-psychological Problem in India', *UPJSSR*, Vol. 1, pp. 11–15.

Jejeebhoy, Shireen J. and Zeba A. Sathar. 2001. 'Women's Autonomy in India and Pakistan: The Influence of Religion and Region', *Population and Development Review*, Vol. 27, No. 4, December, pp. 687–712.

Savanoor, Banashri B. 2009. 'Female Foeticide: Need to Change the Mindset of People', www.legalservicesindia.com, posted on 23 January 2009.

Walia, Ajinder. 2005. 'Female Foeticide in Punjab: Exploring the Socio-economic and Cultural Dimensions', *Idea: A Journal of Social Sciences*, Vol. 10, No. 1, August, www.ideajournal.com/articles.php

8

Ensuring Dignity of the Girl Child

A Case Study of URMUL Initiative in Sri Ganganagar District of Rajasthan

Jaya Kritika Ojha and Binod Mishra

The feudalistic pattern of society in Rajasthan a few decades ago had clear-cut notions about importance of the male child. There have been many stories that have filtered through generations about the humiliation a family had to bear if a girl child was born. They were supposed to be inferior in society, the ones who would go to beg from others the hand of their sons to marry off the daughters. The birth of a girl child was, and is still referred to, in sayings like *Bhaato Aigyo* – a stone has come, or *Bhaato Janam Gayo* – a stone has been born, *chanvari mandgi, moonch neechi hogyi* – the moustache has lowered down. *Beti ka baap* (father of a girl) is a phrase that is still commonly used to refer to a person who is supposed to be helpless, weak, a beggar, a borrower. It meant: 'you have become the father of a daughter and now you must realise your position.' Such phrases are very common in society that is male dominant, patriarchal, and had double sets of values and code conducts, one for men and the other for women.

The secondary position of women has lessened their status in terms of their rights, importance and equality. They have no say, no voice, they cannot decide for themselves. This has endangered not only women's status but also their lives, their right to be born and to live. The progress is anti-women if it does not ensure their right to be born, to live, to exist. The most barbarous practice, our modern society with all its developmental flags, witnesses is determining and destroying the female foetus. The widespread availability of high-tech portable ultrasound machines has outreach to the remote villages too and is an easy way to kill the female foetus. Unfortunately, because there are so many contributors to the problem, varieties of approaches are required to combat female foeticide.

Background

The trend of 'missing girls' has been established through the last two census data of 1991 and 2001. The Census of India 2011 has also revealed the alarming fact of continuous decline of sex ratio. In Rajasthan, the sex ratio in the age-group of 0–6 years shows a continuous decline from 954 in 1981 to 916 in 1991 and 909 in 2001. The continuously declining sex ratio in Rajasthan has become a matter of concern since it augurs serious consequences about the overall development of the state in the years to come. The district of Sri Ganganagar is the worst hit with a girl child sex ratio of 850 girls to 1,000 boys in the 0–6 year age group.

Despite a law against sex selection, detecting the sex of the unborn foetus and then aborting it because it is female has been accorded a silent social sanction as a private matter of couples and families. The challenge in the new millennium is to convince the communities to change the deeply internalized mindsets against the girl child and to uphold and honour a value system that serves to eliminate gender bias. In such a scenario, only a change in mindsets towards establishing the value of the girl child would lead to stopping discriminatory practices against the girl child, the most heinous act being the pre-birth elimination of females.

Once the girl child is allowed to be born, she must also be given the right to live a life of dignity. The needs of female children for rearing, nutrition, health, education and survival need to be addressed by influencing and changing the mindset of their parents and other care-takers through community gate-keepers and the existing service delivery points like health, integrated child development services, education, youth development through community-based responses (CBR).

Objectives

1. To study the situation of sex discrimination in Rajasthan.
2. To understand the role of URMUL organization as a catalyst against female foeticide in Rajasthan.
3. To emphasize the involvement of community, media, students and government functionaries in creating awareness regarding the girl child.

Western Rajasthan is a land of desert. It is a sandy, harsh and unfriendly terrain. Ganganagar is the most developed and productive district of western Rajasthan. The total population of Ganganagar district is 1,789,423, with male population of 9,55,378 and female population of 8,34,045. Density of population is 224 per km^2. The literacy rate is 64.74 per cent (2001 Census). This is one of the most prosperous districts not only of Rajasthan but also of India. But in this district, the female to male gender ratio, according to the 2001 Census of India, is 872:1,000, which indicates the lowest number of girls in the region.

In Thar Desert of Rajasthan, a developmental organization 'URMUL' is doing pioneering work to combat female foeticide in the rural and urban areas of Ganganagar, Hanumangarh and Jaisalmer districts of western Rajasthan.

URMUL, the Organization

URMUL is a well-known voluntary agency working in western Rajasthan for the last 22 years in the field of rural development, especially on the issue of reproductive and child health. The URMUL Rural Health, Research and

Development Trust, Bikaner, was initiated by URMUL Dairy (Uttari Rajasthan Cooperative Milk Union Ltd.), Bikaner long back in 1983.

URMUL's Initiative for Ensuring Dignity of the Girl Child in Sri Ganganagar District of Rajasthan

Realizing the challenging issue of female foeticide, URMUL took the social responsibility to work against girl child discrimination through the awareness generation projects to stop female foeticide. 'URMUL', with their regular efforts and interventions, have made a visible positive change in people's attitudes towards the girl child and strengthening community-based responses to combat female sex selection and to establish the dignity of the girl child in Rajasthan.

The organization followed a two-pronged approach:

- Sensitization and mobilization of the community on the issue of female foeticide in selected areas of Sri Ganganagar with the lowest child sex ratio.
- Generating awareness and supporting implementation of the PCPNDT Act (Pre-Conception and Pre-Natal Diagnostics Technique Act) at the district level.

URMUL as a facilitator, actor and change agent coordinates with the government functionaries, and community opinion leaders, resource groups, financial and physical supporters. The target population for these community-based interventions are women, men, youth, adolescents and school children in the selected villages. The project reached out to key decision-makers in the family (older men and women) and the community (caste/religious leaders, village elders, panchayat members) for bringing about change in the value system that is required to end foeticide. Special focus was placed on families who have female children less than six years of age and pregnant women.

The capacity and motivation of the frontline village health workers and community leaders was increased through trainings/orientations, monitoring and support mechanisms. The outreach activities were based on

Behaviour Change Communication (BCC) methods. The interventions used a 'life cycle' approach by the health care providers and community gate-keepers.

This intervention has made a positive difference in the knowledge, attitude and practices of people. This momentum at the community-level needs to be sustained and expanded to promote full community ownership and sustainability and increase the visibility of the issue.

In addition, millennia old practices are being challenged and small but significant steps towards establishing the value of the girl child are being made at the level of the community, local governance and the district and state administration.

Important Role of Media, Students and Information-Communication Material in the Movement

Rajasthan Patrika and *Dainik Bhaskar*, the two leading newspapers, along with locally published newspapers give a large coverage to the activities against female foeticide, appreciate the efforts made by the active participants in the movement and use their influence against those who are engaged in malpractices. Media gives a good coverage of the steps to recognize and honour parents of newborn girls. As such, the role of media is very important for multiplication of efforts on the issue of dignity of girl child, reducing atrocities, and spreading awareness regarding importance in keeping girls alive/giving birth to girl child, to ensure the rights of girls.

URMUL Promotes Kanya Lohri

Lohri is a winter harvest festival celebrated in Punjab and the first *Lohri* for male children is celebrated with pomp and gaiety. Sesame sweets, peanuts and lump of jaggery are offered into a large bonfire to seek blessings for the longevity and good health of the infant son. Contrary to custom, URMUL promoted a *Lohri* function organized for daughters born in Sri Ganganagar, a practice hitherto reserved for boys.

For the first time in the history of the city, a celebration of Kanya (girl child) Lohri at Sri Ganganagar was held on 13 January 2008. Despite market recession in 2009, the city once again held a *Kanya Lohri* celebration for the second year in succession and honoured 51 baby girls, who were still in their first year of life, before a 5,000-strong crowd.

Additionally, in January 2010, on the occasion of the third *Kanya Lohri* celebration, the Sri Ganganagar Chamber of Commerce announced scholarships worth 2,20,000 USD (INR 10,00,000) for girls from families with one or two daughters and no son. These scholarships included financial support in the form of tuition waiver for higher studies, including professional courses like engineering, laboratory technology, physiotherapy, nursing, and dental surgery, etc.

Efforts are underway to institute this intervention by the people of Sri Ganganagar as a yearly event. On the 13 January 2011, *Kanya Lohri* was celebrated on a very large scale, jointly by URMUL Trust, community and Chamber of Commerce of Ganganagar.

Conclusion

Ganganagar in Rajasthan, being the most prosperous district of the state, also reported as the worst-hit district with a girl child sex ratio of 850 girls to 1,000 boys in the 0–6 year age group. Realizing the urgency towards this burning issue, developmental organizations like URMUL Trust with the support of media channels, school-colleges, village panchayats, chamber of commerce and state administration is doing pioneering work to combat female foeticide in the rural and urban areas of Ganganagar, Hanumangarh and Jaisalmer districts of western Rajasthan. They are spreading awareness messages, people are now celebrating *Kanya Lohri* and the couples who have girl children are publically honoured for their decision. URMUL Trust and the community members are happy for their efforts of raising voices against female foeticide in the region because of the recent figures of the Census 2011, which shows a slight improvement in the numbers of female child in the district.

References

Census of India. 2001. Retrieved on 12 September 2010, from www.censusindia.net/

Harper, M. 1998. *The New Middle Women: Profitable Banking Through Lending Groups*, New Delhi: Oxford and IBH Publishing.

http://ganganagar.nic.in/ Retrieved on 10 September 2010.

http://nipccd.nic.in/reports/racl.pdf Retrieved on 10 September 2010.

http://pndt.gov.in/writereaddata/mainlinkfile/File22.pdf Retrieved on 12 September 2010.

http://pndt.gov.in/writereaddata/mainlinkfile/File99.pdf Retrieved on 12 September 2010.

http://rajswasthya.nic.in/PCPNDT%20Workshop/Sex%20Ratio%20(06)%20Final/Akhilesh%20sex%20ratio%2016.12.pdf Retrieved on 10 September 2010.

MOHFW. 2005. 'Annual Report on Implementation of the Pre-Conception and Pre-Natal Diagnostic Techniques (Prohibition of Sex Selection) Act', PNDT Division, Ministry of Health and Family Welfare, Government of India, New Delhi.

Nanda, A.R. 2010. 'Advocacy Papers on Population Issues', Population Foundation of India.

Rajasthan Human Development Report (RHDR). 2002. Retrieved on 12 September 2008, from http://data.undp.org.in/shdr/raj/rajhdr.pdf.

Sample Registration System. 2009. *Bulletin Registrar General*, Vol. 44, No. 1, Vital Statistics Division, New Delhi.

9

Combating Female Foeticide

PCPNDT Act and Its Implementation

Mitu Khurana

Sex ratios, which are defined as number of females per 1,000 males in a population, have been constantly declining in many parts of India, particularly in the states of Haryana, Punjab, Delhi and Odisha. According to International Development Research Center (IDRC), 2001 Census of India revealed that the proportion of girls aged 0–6 years had further dropped from 945:1,000 to 927:1,000 since the 1991 Census.

The PNDT Act was passed in 1994, and PNDT rules were passed in 1996, with an aim to check this alarming trend of decrease in the number of females in the Indian society. The rules were passed to aid in the implementation of the Act. The Act was modified in 2002 so as to include pre-conception techniques which could selectively stop the conception of the female foetuses by segregating X and Y carrying sperms. The PCPNDT rules were modified in 2003. Despite the PCPNDT Act being a very strong piece of legislation, it has failed to curb the menace of female foeticide. The sex ratios of almost all states of India continue to decline.

According to the Delhi government website, the sex ratio scenario of Delhi is as follows:

Table 1

Female to Male Sex Ratio

Place	*1991 Census*	*2001 Census*
India	927	933
Delhi	827	821

The news article 'Skewed Sex Ratio May Fuel Unrest, Says Study', which appeared in *Hindustan Times* on 4 September 2010, tells about a report of Ministry of Statistics and Programme Implementation – Men and Women in India, 2010 – which found that the proportion of girls in the 0–14 age group of the total population of women which was 33 per cent in 2005 had fallen to 31.9 per cent in 2008. In case of boys, the proportion in the 0–14 age group of the total population of men had increased from 31.8 per cent in 2008 to 32.5 per cent in 2008. This report said that in 1991, 105 boys were born for every 100 girls born, which increased to 107 in 2001 and 112 in 2009.

The PCPNDT Act 1994 provides for:

- Prohibition of sex selection, before and after conception (Section 3A of the Act)
- Regulation of pre-natal diagnostic techniques (e.g. amniocentesis and ultrasonography) for detection of genetic abnormalities, by restricting their use to registered institutions. The Act allows the use of these techniques only at a registered place for a specified purpose and by a qualified person, registered for this purpose (Section 4 of the Act)
- Prevention of misuse of such techniques for sex selection before or after conception (Section 6 of the Act)
- Prohibition of advertisement of any technique for sex selection as well as sex determination (Section 22 of the Act)

- Prohibition on sale of ultrasound machines to persons not registered under this Act (Rule 3A, inserted vide GSR, 109 (e) Dt. 14 January 2003)
- Punishment for violation of provisions of the Act (Section 23)

Table 2

PNDT Act Violations

Non-availability of copy of the PNDT Act in the registered centre	Case may be launched in the court of JMIC under section 25 of the Act Show-cause notice u/s 20(1),(2) for temporary suspension of registration.
Non-display of registration certificate in the centre	
Non-display of Board on the premises in English and local language	
Advertisement relating to pre-conception and pre-natal determination of sex	U/s 22(3) of the PNDT Amendment Act, case is to be launched in the court u/s 28 of the Act.
Unregistered centres/machine	Equipment to be sealed and seized by the appropriate authority concerned. Launch the case in the court u/s 28 of the Act. Registration granted after penalty and affidavit.
Record-keeping irregularities in record keeping as per revised form 'F' is a major offence	Contravention (a major offence) of provisions of section 5 and 6 of the Act and punishable u/s 23(1) of the PNDT Act.
Sex selection	Violation of section 5 and 6 of the Act and punishable u/s 23 of the Act.

Under the Act, any case where the diagnostic procedure is done but the records are not properly maintained is presumed to be a case of sex selection unless contrary is proved by the doctor conducting the procedures. Every setup registered under the Act has to submit before the fifth of every month the prescribed forms of all procedures done in the preceding month to the Chief District Medical Officer, who is the appropriate authority under the Act.

A Full Bench of Gujarat High Court in the case 'Suo Motu Vs State of Gujarat' on 30 September 2008 made the observations that any improper maintenance of record in itself is equivalent to violation of the provisions of the Act. The Bench of Judges also observed that cases where Form F is not filled at all, or where the vital details are lacking, such that the woman who has undergone the ultrasound cannot be identified, then this lapse cannot be passed over as a procedural lapse, and has to be in all seriousness tried in a court of law. Therefore, any clinic not maintaining proper records is required to be exposed to proceedings under Section 23 of the Act.

Conducting pre-natal diagnostic test procedures in an establishment which is not registered under the Act: In the case of *Centre for Enquiry into Health and Allied Themes (CEHAT) and Others Vs Union of India and Others (2003) Rd-Sc 444* (September 2003), the Supreme Court of India gave directions to appropriate authorities that those establishments which are not registered under the Act are required to be prosecuted by the authorities under the provisions of the Act and there is no question of issue of warning and to permit them to continue their illegal activities. The Supreme Court also ordered that in case a clinic or establishment is conducting pre-natal diagnostic techniques without registration, the appropriate authorities or any officer of the Central or the state government authorized on its behalf is required to file a complaint under Section 28 of the Act for prosecuting the offenders.

Review of Literature

According to UNFPA, six Asian countries (India, South Korea, Georgia, Azerbaijan, China and Armenia) reported a severe sex-ratio imbalance in 2005, with estimated overall sex ratio in India being 107.5 males per 100 females, as against 106.8 in China, 106 in Pakistan and 104.9 in Bangladesh.

The government of South Korea banned sex-determination tests in 1987 (reinforced in 1994). In 1991, it also launched mass media campaigns. Along with these, there was a change in the scenario because of exceptional economic growth lasting 20 years, which contributed to increasing women's autonomy.

The Chinese government took some steps to combat the practice of female infanticide and sex-selective abortion of female foetuses. China employed the 'Marriage Law' and 'Women's Protection Law', both of which prohibit female infanticide. The 'Women's Protection Law' also prohibits any form of discrimination against 'women who give birth to female babies'. The 'Maternal Health Care Law of 1994' strictly prohibits the use of technology to identify the gender of a foetus.

The Indian government passed the Pre-Conception and Pre-Natal Diagnostic Test Act. Despite this Act being passed, sex ratios have been continuously declining in the past decades.

The Supreme Court of India, while disposing of a Public Interest Litigation of CEHAT and Others Vs Union of India and Others in 2001, made the observation that it was very clear that to a large extent that the Central government or the state governments were not implementing the PNDT Act.

Nine years after this observation of the Supreme Court, the scenario has still not changed much as is evident from the newspaper article which appeared in *The Times of India* on 21 July 2010, titled 'UP Still Not Serious on PCPNDT Act'. This article shows how even after nine years, despite the sex ratio continually declining in the state, the state government of Uttar Pradesh is not seriously implementing the PCPNDT Act.

The same news item reported how the authorities went about prosecuting the violators of the Act in the state of Uttar Pradesh. The district administration of Jaunpur dropped the drive which it launched from 27 March to 1 April in 2010 to catch the various violators of the act; the drive so initiated was dropped due to political pressure. Later, registration of some establishments was cancelled/operation suspended for variable periods or they were let-off with only a warning. No legal action such as filing of court case under the PCPNDT Act was taken by the administration. Even during raids conducted in June 2009 by the state inspection and monitoring committee in Kaushambi, no action was taken despite the fact that lapses were found in several ultrasound and diagnostic establishments.

According to Annual Report on Implementation of PNDT Act 2006, till March 2006, the highest number of ongoing cases was registered in Delhi (76), followed by Punjab (72) and Gujarat (57).

However, National Support and Monitoring Cell gave a five month (15 May – 14 October 2006) activity report in October of 2006 after analysing the implementation of the Act in various states. They found that in Delhi there was no list of the 81 complaints/prosecutions supposedly launched by the state authorities. Court cases were supposedly launched only against 3 out of 35 unregistered establishments found during raids. There were no details available on the status of these 3 court cases also.

There were 46 more complaints in which the state authorities were supposed to initiate action. Out of these 46, in one clinic registration had been cancelled, in one clinic fine was imposed of ₹ 15,000 only. Court cases were launched against 19 cases, out of which 8 cases were later withdrawn at various stages.

They gave the conclusion that in Delhi, there is:

- Neither transparency nor clarity in the functioning of the authorities authorized under the PNDT Act.
- Wrong reporting regarding the number of court cases filed.
- Lack of accountability and will to enforce the law.
- The state is totally complacent on the issue, and there is no monitoring of actions prescribed in the Act.
- A total irresponsible reporting in flagrant violation of norms, rules and regulations.

The news article 'Here, Blue Still Wins Over Pink' appearing in *The Times of India* on 5 August 2010 quotes a ministry report that as on 21 April 2008, there were 420 ongoing court/police cases in India for violations of the law. Out of these 420 cases, only 65 cases are due to identification and sex determination of the foetus, 43 are for advertisements regarding facilities for sex selection and 312 are for non-registration of clinics/facilities.

First three court cases under this Act were filed in the state of Haryana. The first conviction in PNDT case in the country was also in the state of Haryana. Further, 14 doctors/persons have been convicted, 115 ultrasound machines have been seized and sealed and 245 ultrasound establishments had their registration suspended/cancelled in state of Haryana. About 1,036 ultrasound clinics/genetic establishments and 67 genetic counselling establishments and 42 ultrasound machines in the government sector are registered in Haryana.

One doctor was convicted in Ahmedabad in February of 2009 for not submitting the monthly records regularly every month to the appropriate authority.

Objectives

To study the action taken against the guilty under the PCPNDT Act by the implementing authorities (i.e. the Chief District Medical Officer – CDMO) in Delhi, through the data got through an RTI application, we analysed:

- District-wise breakup of establishments against whom action was taken under the PCPNDT Act from March 2008 to March 2010.
- District-wise breakup of the offences under the PCPNDT Act from March 2008 to March 2010.
- Offence-wise breakup of the punishment given to the establishments for violating the provisions of PCPNDT Act from March 2008 to March 2010.

Data and Method

For the purpose of this study, we analysed the secondary data, i.e. a reply received by Mrs Manju of IIT, New Delhi by means of an RTI (filed in March 2010) through which she obtained information from the Director, PNDT cell, Delhi state, regarding:

- Establishments raided and sealed in past two years,
- offences for which they were sealed,
- their status at time of giving reply to RTI,
- if open, the action taken after which the establishments were de-sealed, and
- number of court cases filed in state of Delhi in the past two years under the PCPNDT Act.

We did an in-depth study of the data available to us, along with a quantitative study of the replies given of various districts and then entered the data of each district into a table form as follows:

S. No.	*Name of Establishment*	*Offence*	*Action Taken*	*Present Status*

Our research team did the district-wise data entry as above. After getting the compiled data, we did the data analysis and then derived the following results.

We analysed all the data received by CDMOs of the nine districts of Delhi regarding the action taken by them under the PCPNDT Act.

Findings

After analysing the data available to us, we found that the district-wise breakup of the establishments found violating the PCPNDT was as follows:

Table 3

No. of Establishments Against Whom Action was Initiated

District	*No. of Establishments*
East	82
West	31
South	21
North	45
Central	8
North–East	9
North–West	199
South–West	9
New Delhi	0
Total	404

Figure 1

No. of Establishments Against Whom Action was Initiatied

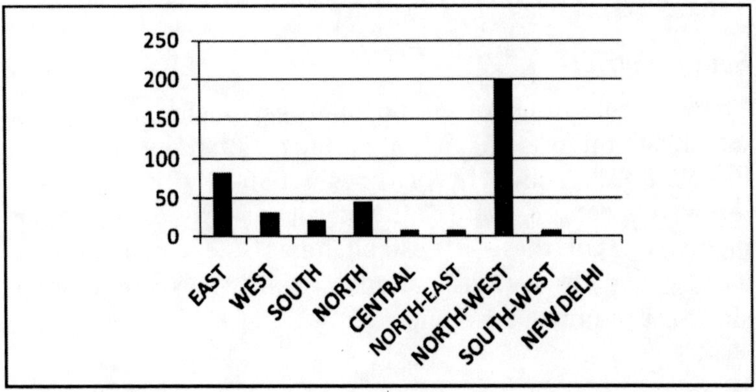

South-West District

There were total of 9 hospitals/clinic in which violation of various provisions of PCPNDT Act was found. However, the exact nature of violation is unknown because it was not mentioned in the reply of RTI. Out of these 9 clinics, show-cause notice was issued to all and only one court case was filed. The reasons for filing the single court case were not specified. Three establishments out of the 8 establishments which were sealed were desealed after paying a penalty and after submitting an affidavit. Three establishments out of the 8 sealed establishments were desealed only after a strict warning by the appropriate authority. The present status and the final action taken against 2 more of the 8 sealed establishments are not mentioned in the RTI.

Table 4

Action Taken in South–West District (Total Establishments: 9)

Show-Cause Notice and Sealed		*Court Case*	
Open	Closed	Open	Closed
8	0	0	1

How were the Sealed Centres Opened		
Penalty+ Affidavit	Strict Warning Only	Unknown
3	3	2

South District

There were a total of 21 hospitals/establishments against which action was taken for various violations under the PCPNDT Act. The RTI reply does not specify the violations for which actions were initiated against the 21 establishments. Out of these 21 establishments, 5 establishments were sealed for various periods. To all 21 establishments, show-cause notice was issued.

Table 5

Action Taken in South District (Total Establishments: 21)

Show-Cause Notice + Sealing		*Only Show-Cause Notice*	
5		16	
Open	Closed	Open	Closed
5	0	16	0
Offence Not Mentioned Under Reply to RTI			

The sealed establishments were desealed after the relief was given to them by the advisory committee and the State Appropriate Authority. According to the reply given in the RTI, all establishments were issued warnings and are under strict surveillance.

West District

There were a total of 31 hospitals/establishments against which action was initiated for violating the provisions of PCPNDT Act. All the 31 establishments were found to be not keeping the records properly, or not submitting the monthly reports to the appropriate authority. Out of these 31 establishments, 4 establishments were sealed. Out of these 4 establishments, 3 were desealed after taking a penalty and an affidavit, while 1 centre was desealed after taking penalty only. A show-cause notice was issued against the other 27 establishments. No further action was taken against the 27 establishments that were issued show-cause notices. Presently, all the 31 are still running.

Table 6

Action Taken in West District (Total Establishments: 31)

	Show-Cause Notice and Sealing		*Only Show-Cause Notice*
If Sealed How Open	Penalty +Affidavit	Penalty	27
	3	1	
Not Keeping Records Properly and not Submitting Monthly Records to the Authorities.			

East District

There were a total of 82 hospitals/establishments that were found violating the PCPNDT Act. Out of these 82, 38 establishments were indulging in non-submission/incomplete submission of Form F, 7 establishments had applied late for renewal of registration (out of which 2 were issued show-cause notice, 1 was sealed, action taken against 2 is not unknown and 2 applied for cancellation and are closed); in 2 establishments, there was no radiologist available, 2 establishments were not registered under the Act, in 2 establishments sting operation were carried out and they showed sex determination being done.

Table 7

Action Taken in East District (Total Establishments: 82)

Offence	*Court Case*	*Registration Cancelled*	*Only Show-Cause Notice*
Record Keeping 38	3	(4)+Suspended in 1	36
Late Application 7	1 Sealed, 2 Closed on Self-Application, Action Against 2 Unknown 0	0	2
No Radiologist 2	2	0	0
Unregistered Centre 2	Action Taken Unknown		
Sting Operations 2	Action Taken Unknown		
Deficiencies in Routine Inspection 22	2 Centres Closed On Self Application		20
Unregistered Machine 1	Action Taken Unknown		

One centre was found which was running an unregistered machine. Other than this, in 22 establishments, various deficiencies were found during routine inspection out of which 2 of these establishments are closed, and others are functioning.

Out of these, 38 establishments found not keeping records properly, registration was cancelled in 4 cases and suspended in 1 centre. Court cases were filed against 3 establishments for not keeping records properly. All 5 establishments are closed/sealed till date. Other than these, 2 more establishments are sealed having their registrations suspended because there was no radiologist working in these establishments. Action taken against the 2 establishments found doing sex determination during sting operations, and the 2 unregistered establishments is not known. The action taken against 1 centre with unregistered machine is also unknown. The registration of 9 establishments was cancelled on self-application. In all other cases, only show-cause notice was issued and no further action taken.

Central District

There were a total of 8 hospitals/establishments against which action was initiated under the PCPNDT Act. Out of these 8 hospitals, action was initiated against 7 establishments for not maintaining records properly and against 1 hospital for unregistered machine. A show-cause notice was issued to all 8 hospitals. Only 1 machine was sealed (where there was an unregistered machine), but even that was opened later after considering the reply to the show-cause notice. All other establishments were only given warnings. Presently all the hospitals/establishments are in a running state.

Table 8

Action Taken in Central District (Total Establishments: 8)

Offence	*Action*	
	Show-Cause Notice	*Sealing*
Deficiencies in Records	7	0
Unregistered Machine	0	1

North District

There were a total of 45 hospitals/establishments found violating various provisions of PCPNDT Act in the North

District. Out of these, 10 establishments were found having incomplete Form F, 9 establishments were not maintaining records properly, in 12 establishments referral slips were not maintained properly with Form F, in 6 establishments Form F was not being submitted, in 4 establishments a radiologist was not available, 1 centre was closed, in 2 establishments PNDT book was not available at reception, in 1 centre the board was not displayed and in 2 establishments the machine was unregistered. Four establishments were not maintaining the compulsory registers. In many establishments, more than one violation was found.

Table 9

Action Taken in North District (Total Establishments: 45)

Offence	*Total*	*Action*	
		Show-Cause Notice	*Sealing*
Incomplete Form F	10	10	0
Improper Records	9	9	0
No Referral Slips	12	12	0
Form F Not Submitted	6	6	0
No Radiologist	4	2	2
Book Unavailable	2	2	0
Board Not Displayed	1	1	0
Machine Unregistered	2	2	0
No Register Maintained	4	4	0

Show-cause notices were issued to 43 and 2 were sealed. One clinic was closed and registration cancelled. For the 2 establishments which were sealed, this action was taken because no radiologist was working there, and this fact had not been intimated to the appropriate authorities.

Presently 42 establishments are running, 2 establishments are sealed and one is closed.

North–West District

There were a total of 199 hospitals/establishments against which action was initiated in the past 2 years for various violations of PCPNDT Act. About 151 establishments did not submit Form F for various periods of time ranging from 1 month to 10 months and 48 establishments did late submission of Form F. Show-cause notice was issued to all 199 establishments. Out of these 199, at present only 2 are closed and 197 are still running.

Table 10

Action Taken in North–West District (Total Establishments: 199)

Offence	*Action*	
	Show-Cause Notice	*Sealing*
Late Submission	48	0
Non-Submission	151	0

North–East District

Five establishments were sealed in the last 2 years in North–East district. Out of these 5, 2 establishments were sealed because there was no qualified doctor in the centre, 2 were sealed following complaints of sex determination after a sting operation by a journalist, and 1 was sealed due to expiry of registration. All the 5 establishments are sealed till date, and a court case has been filed against all of the above mentioned clinics.

Other than these, 4 more establishments were issued show-cause notices in the last 2 years (1 for no referral slips with Form F, and incomplete Form F, 1 for doing ultrasound tests from an unregistered machine, 1 for doing ultrasound from a registered machine, but at an unregistered place, and 1 for expiry of registration).

Table 11

Action Taken in North–East District (Total Establishments: 9)

Offence	*Total*	*Action*	
		Show-Cause Notice	*Sealing*
No Qualified Doc	2	0	2
Sting Operation	2	0	2
Registration Exp	1	0	1
No Referral Slips	1	1	0
Incomplete Form F	1	1	0
Unregistered Machine	1	1	0
Unregistered Centre	1	1	0

New Delhi District

In New Delhi district, no action was taken against any clinic in the past 2 years. No clinic was issued a show-cause notice, neither was any court case filed in the past 2 years. No clinic in New Delhi district was found violating the provisions of PCPNDT Act.

Table 12

Offence-Wise Analysis

Offence	*Total*	*%*
Non-submission of Monthly Records	157	38.29268
Deficiency in Record Keeping	112	27.31707
Late Submission of Monthly Records	48	11.70732
Unknown	31	7.560976
No Referral Slips	14	3.414634
Incomplete Form F	12	2.926829
No Qualified Doctor	10	2.439024
No Register Maintained	4	0.97561
Registration Expired	6	1.463415
Unregistered Machine	7	1.707317
Book Unavailable	2	0.487805
Sting Operation	4	0.97561
Board Not Displayed	1	0.243902
Unregistered Place	2	0.487805

Out of 404 establishments found violating various provisions of PCPNDT Act, 12 establishments (2.9%) were filling incomplete Form F, 112 establishments (27.3%) were not keeping records properly, 48 (11.7%) were submitting monthly report late to the appropriate authorities, 7 establishments (1.7%) had machines unregistered, 2 establishments (0.4%) were unregistered and 6 centres (1.4%) had expired registration. Four (0.97%) establishments were found indulging in sex determination and unqualified persons were running the establishment in 10 establishments (2.4%).

Offence-Wise Action – Show-Cause Notice/Sealed/Court Case: While analysing the data to see the action for the different offences, we have not counted the centres for which the action taken was not known.

Table 13

Offence-Wise Action

Offence	*Show-Cause Notice*	*Sealed*	*Court Case*	*Total*
Non-submission of Monthly Records	157	0	0	157
Deficiency in Record Keeping	109	0	3	112
Late Submission of Monthly Records	48	0	0	48
Unknown	30	0	1	31
No Referral Slips	13	1	0	14
Incomplete Form F	11	1	0	12
No Qualified Doctor	4	2	4	10
No Register Maintained	4	0	0	4
Registration Expired	4	1	1	6
Unregistered Machine	4	3	0	7
Book Unavailable	2	0	0	2
Sting Operation	2	0	2	4
Board Not Displayed	1	0	0	1
Unregistered Place	1	1	0	2

- *Non-submission of monthly records:* 157 centres were not submitting the monthly records to appropriate authorities for a period ranging from 2 months to 10 months. Only show-cause notice was issued to all the centres which were not submitting the monthly records.
- *Not maintaining records properly:* 112 establishments were found not maintaining Form F properly. Out of these, 109 centres were issued only a show-cause notice and no further action was taken against them. There were 3 court cases for not maintaining records properly.
- *Late submission of Form F:* 48 establishments were observed submitting Form F late. A show-cause notice was issued to all 48 establishments and no further action was taken against them.
- *Not maintaining referral slips with Form F:* 14 establishments were found not attaching the referral slips with the monthly records. One centre was sealed, and 13 were issued only a show-cause notice.
- *Incomplete Form F:* action was initiated against 12 establishments in Delhi in the last 2 years for incomplete Form F. All the 11 establishments found not filling Form F properly were given a show-cause notice, and remained open. They are still open and functioning.
- *No qualified doctor available in the establishment:* There were 10 establishments where there was no qualified radiologist/doctor available. Four of these centres were issued only show-cause notice, 2 were sealed and court case was filed against 4 establishments.
- *No register maintained:* There were 4 centres found not maintaining the mandatory register showing the list of women who had come for pre-natal tests. All the 4 centres were issued only a show-cause notice and no further action was taken against them.
- *Registration expiry/late application for renewal:* 6 centres had an expired registration and had either not applied for renewal or had applied late. Show-cause notice was issued to 4 of them, while 1 centre was sealed and in only 1 case a court case was registered.

- *Unregistered machine:* 7 establishments were doing pre-natal diagnostic testing on unregistered machines or during raid it was found that the machine had a different serial number than the one that was registered. Four establishments having unregistered machines were issued show-cause notice, but are open and no further action was initiated against them. Three centres were sealed, but are open now. No court case has been lodged.
- *Sex determination, including sting operations:* 4 establishments in Delhi were found conducting sex determination tests. However, a court case was filed against only 2 of them. The action taken against the other 2 is not known as the answer was not given in the RTI.
- *Unregistered centre:* There were 2 unregistered establishments conducting pre-natal diagnostic tests. One centre was sealed and one was issued a show-cause notice. No court case was lodged.
- *Closed on self-application:* 9 establishments are closed on self-application for closure.
- *Nature of offence unknown:* 31 establishments have been mentioned in the reply to the RTI, where the offence is not mentioned, but the action taken is mentioned. Out of these, 30 establishments were issued show-cause notice, while 1 court case has been registered.

Table 14

Only Show-Cause Notice Given and No Further Action Initiated

Offence	*Total*	*Only Show-Cause Notice*	*%*
Late Submission	48	48	100
Unknown	31	30	96.77
No Referral Slips	14	13	92.85
Incomplete Form F	12	11	91.66
No Qualified Doctor	10	4	40
No Register Maintained	4	4	100

Cont'd...

...Cont'd

Registration Expired	6	4	66.66
Unregistered Machine	7	4	57.14
Book Unavailable	2	2	100
Sting Operation	4	2	50
Board Not Displayed	1	1	100
Unregistered Place	2	1	50
Non Submission of Monthly Records	157	157	100
Deficiency in Record Keeping	112	109	97.32
	410	390	95.12

Observations

By doing the above analysis of the data, we have come to the following conclusions:

- The PCPNDT Act is not being implemented by the authorities in the state of Delhi in the true spirit.
- The establishments found not keeping the records properly are being let off by giving them a simple show-cause notice.
- The authorities are letting off the establishments sealed for improper record keeping by taking simple penalty and an affidavit.
- In violation of orders of the Supreme Court of India, in case of 8 establishments (6 unregistered machines +unregistered establishments), no court case was filed.
- The maximum number of offenders were in North–West District of Delhi, while in the New Delhi District no establishment was found violating the provisions of PCPNDT Act.
- Only 11 establishments of the 404 establishments have been prosecuted under Section 23/28 and have court cases registered against them.

Recommendations

- The CDMOs should be made accountable for sex ratios of their districts.

- Proper scrutiny should be done that whether the CDMOs are taking action as per the PCPNDT Act and subsequent judgments of Supreme Court and High Courts or not against the violating clinics.
- Legal action should be initiated against CDMOs who are trying to protect the guilty under the Act/letting the guilty go scot-free with minimum punishment.
- The National Inspection and Monitoring Committee should have a regulatory role over the legal actions being initiated against the clinics/establishments raided by them.
- The media should be involved in all raids, so that no complaint can be swept under the carpet by the implementing authorities.
- Software for computerization of Form F should be developed. Through this software, the machine must be regulated so that only after Form F is filled can an obstetric ultrasound be performed. Form F so filled can be directly submitted to a central server which collects all Form Fs for the state.
- Medical audit of scanning centres by analysing the data submitted by them in Form 'F' through software should be outsourced to independent NGOs. Based on the medical audit report; necessary disciplinary action be taken not only against scanning centre that indulges in malpractice and does not comply with the rules, but also the appropriate authorities in whose area the offence is taking place.
- At District and State level, a strong vigil is needed through the involvement of NGOs at the field level.
- The lighter provisions of the penalty and affidavit which have been provided for unregistered establishments in PCPNDT rules should be scrapped.

It is a known fact that sex ratios have been continuously declining. The PCPNDT Act was passed to check this decline in the sex ratios, which could result in a social catastrophe. However, because of poor implementation of the Act, it has failed to check the heinous crime of female foeticide. The rapidly declining sex ratios in all the districts of Delhi show that there is no fear of the law in the minds of the law-breakers. Therefore, if the government really wants to check the declining sex ratios, it needs to urgently take steps to strictly enforce the Act, so that there is fear in the minds of the law-breakers.

References

Annual Report. 2006 (pndt.gov.in/writereaddata/mainlinkfile/File99.pdf).

Express News Service. 2009. 'Doctor Convicted for Violating PNDT Act', 4 February (http://www.indianexpress.com/news/doctor-convicted-for-violating-pndt-act/418997/).

Five Month Activity Report of National Support and Monitoring Cell from 15 May–14 October 2006 (mohfw.nic.in/.../NSMC/NSMC%20Activity%20Report_May-Oct%2006.pdf).

Gorea, R.K. 2004. 'Editorial', *JIAFM*, Vol. 26, No. 3.

Guilmoto, Christophe Z. 2007. *Sex-ratio Imbalance in Asia: Trends, Consequences and Policy Responses*, Paris: United Nations Population Fund.

Health Department of Haryana. 'Implementation of PNDT Act 1994 in Haryana' (http://haryanahealth.nic.in/menudesc.aspx?Page=2).

Jones, A. 1999. 'Case Study: Female Infanticide', Gendercide Watch (http://www.gendercide.org/ case_infanticide.html).

——. 'Violations Under the PNDT Act and the Penalties' (http://pndt.gov.in/ index1.asp?linkid=19).

Oberoi, Radhika. 2008. 'Here, Blue Still Wins Over Pink', *The Times of India*, 5 August (http://www.geneticsandsociety.org/article.php?id=4207).

Supreme Court of India. 2001. 'Centre for Enquiry into Health and Allied Themes (CHEHAT) and Ors Vs Union of India and Ors, Writ Petition (Civil) No. 301 of 2000', order dated 4 May.

Times News Network, Lucknow. 2010. 'UP Still Not Serious on PCPNDT Act', 14 July (http://timesofindia.indiatimes.com/city/lucknow/UP-still-not-serious-on-PCPNDT-Act/articleshow/6164935.cms).

10

Female Foeticide

A Silent Violence

Sudha Yadav

Female infanticide has been a common practice in our country for centuries. Indian census has always shown a gendered imbalance. This marked gap between boys and girls, which has nationwide implications, is the result of decisions made at the most local level – the family. Death is a tragedy in whatever form, at whatever time and in whatever way it lays its hands. Female foeticide is a unique form of violence against women and the girl child. Discrimination of a girl child starts even before in the form of sex-determination tests, misusing the high technology of amniocentesis, resulting in a new kind of femicide, i.e. abortion of a female foetus. The birth of a girl is occasioned with sorrow and silence. Even health-wise, these tests can cause a great deal of damage to the foetus. The word 'abortion' has been derived from 'abortus', which means to take away and truly, the practice takes away the wholeness of a woman who resorts to taking away the life of her unborn child. Twin pressures of 'family planning' and 'dowry' have brought female foeticide to such a shameful proportion that sex ratio has been declining fast in India, more so in the states of Punjab, Haryana and Union Territory of Chandigarh.

Female foeticide is a practice that involves the detection of the sex of the unborn baby in the womb of the mother and the decision to abort it if the sex of the child is detected as a girl. This could be done at the behest of the mother, or father, or both or under family pressure. This detection of the sex of the baby is done through three methods:

(a) Amniocentesis;
(b) Chronic Villus Sampling; and
(c) Ultrasonography.

Amniocentesis test is actually a technique for the pre-natal testing of a foetus to detect serious genetic defects sufficiently early in pregnancy so that if needed, the foetus can be aborted. This test is conducted after 16th week of pregnancy. Chronic Villus Sampling is a slightly more technically difficult test than amniocentesis. Its major advantage lies in the fact that it can be performed earlier in the pregnancy (around the 10th week of gestation), thus allowing for an earlier and safer abortion, if desired. This test, similar to amniocentesis, is performed in many clinics and hospitals though it is more costly and is thus utilized chiefly by the wealthy. Ultrasonography is the process of imaging deep structures of the body by measuring and recording the reflection of pulsed or continuous high-frequency sound waves. It is valuable in many medical situations, including the diagnosis of foetal abnormalities, gallstones, heart defects, and tumours.

Historical Background

The killing of women exists in various forms in societies all over the world. However, Indian society displays some unique and particularly brutal versions, such as dowry deaths and Sati. Sex-selective abortion is a fairly recent phenomenon but its root can be traced back to the age-old practice of female infanticide. Sex-selective abortions and increase in the number of female infanticide cases have become a significant social phenomenon in several parts of India. It transcends all castes, class and communities and

Figure 1

Sex Ratio in India

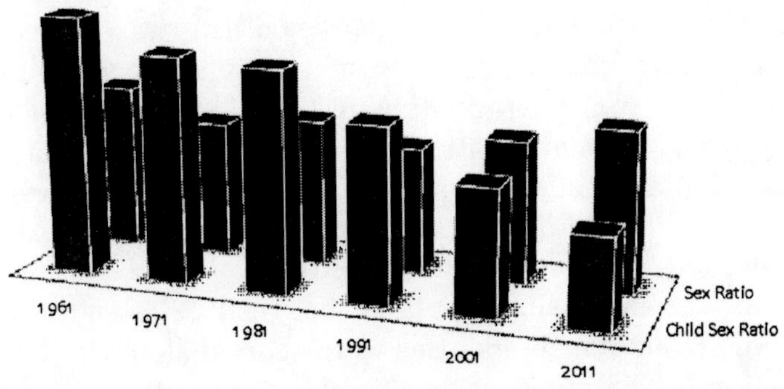

	1961	1971	1981	1991	2001	2011
■ Child Sex Ratio	976	964	962	945	927	914
■ Sex Ratio	941	930	934	927	933	940

even the North–South dichotomy. Female foeticide is an extreme manifestation of violence against women. Female foetuses are selectively aborted after pre-natal sex determination, thus avoiding the birth of girls. As a result of sex-selective abortions, between 35 and 40 million girls and women are missing from the Indian population. The girl children become target of attack even before they are born.

India's 2011 Census shows a serious decline in the number of girls under the age of seven – activists fear eight million female foetuses may have been aborted in the past decade. In 1961, for every 1,000 boys under the age of seven, there were 976 girls. Today, the figure has dropped to a dismal 914 girls. The 2001 and 2011 Censuses registered a significant decline in the CSR across India (18 and 13 point decline, respectively, suggesting that the rate of deterioration was slowing). Daughter disadvantage persists in most parts of the Indian society – though not universally or equally so – and is expressed through sex-selective abortion, neglect of female children, and female infanticide (Sudha and Rajan, 1999).

Amniocentesis was introduced in 1974 'to ascertain birth defects in a sample population', but 'was quickly appropriated by medical entrepreneurs'. Sex determination technologies were soon being marketed as a way to detect unwanted daughters in the womb. It is now commonly known as a sex determination test. In early 1979, North India's first sex determination clinic was opened in Amritsar; soon, similar clinics mushroomed in Punjab, Haryana, Western UP and Maharashtra. Amniocentesis has become popular not only in cities but also in rural areas. Hence, this test became increasingly popular between 1978 and 1982, around 78,000 female foetuses were aborted after sex determination test in our country (*The Times of India*, Editorial, June 1982). Gender preference has its effect on fertility. According to NFHS data (1989–92), the states like Maharashtra, Himachal Pradesh, Gujarat, Punjab and Haryana are making a business through sex determination test and it shows that gender preference has stalled the fertility transition.

Unfortunately, due to availability of the techniques of amniocentesis tests and its 95 to 97 per cent accurate results, not only are the mothers neglected, but even the unborn babies are made to die. Diaz (1988) states that in a well-known abortion centre in Mumbai, after undertaking the sex determination tests, out of the 15,914 abortions performed during 1984–85, almost 100 per cent were those of girl foetuses.

Similarly, a survey report of women's centre in Mumbai found that out of 8,000 foetuses aborted in six city hospitals, 7,999 foetuses were of girls (Gangrade, 1988: 63–70). It is reported that about 4,000 female babies are aborted in Tamil Nadu (southern India) every year. The Maharashtra government had estimated that as many as 45,000 such abortions were carried out in 1985 in the Greater Bombay area alone. Again, the *Indian Express* of 16 September 1986 carried a news item regarding the surveys conducted in one of the leading hospitals of Bombay where out of 1,000 cases, 974 happened to be female foetuses and as such got aborted.

Sex-selective abortion can influence both fertility and sex ratio. A study shows that about 5 per cent of female foetuses are aborted in India on the basis of sex ratio at birth (SRB). For children whose mothers had undergone ultrasound and amniocentesis tests, in Haryana 43 per cent of female foetuses are likely to be aborted for these same women (Arnold et al., 1998). In Punjab and Haryana, these sex-selective abortions increased from 62,000 to 69,000 in Haryana and from 51,000 to 57,000 in Punjab (*The Hindu*, 19 October 2001).

The National Population Policy promotes a two-child norm. The result in family planning acceptors is that amniocentesis and ultrasound tests are used to find out the sex of the unborn child, and female foetuses are increasingly aborted. The small family 'norm' is disposing of daughters. The unborn girl child is most at the risk in the northern states of India. In 1986, media published reports of 78,000 female foetuses aborted in a five-year period (*The Times of India*, June 1986). The National Crime Records Bureau's 2000 report shows a 56.8 per cent rise in female foeticide cases in the five years since 1995, mostly cases of aborting female foetus: If the first birth is female, the next pregnancy has diminished chances of going to full term if the foetus is female (Zheng et al., 1993). Studies show that Punjab is largely geared up to meet family planning targets and female foeticide and sex determination test cases are mostly found in Punjab.

In Haryana, the hoardings proclaim 'Spend 5,000 now or 5 lakh later'. This means to have a girl child is a big burden for the parents and rearing and bearing of girl child is a heavy expense. To keep safe from this burden (girl child), people go to hospitals for the sex determination tests. The phenomena of foeticide of girls seem to be confined to Rajputs, Yadavs and Gujjars in Rajasthan and MP, and the Jats in Punjab and Haryana. Muslims, Scheduled Castes and Scheduled Tribes have a much better sex ratio in these states. The rates of female foeticide are high in rural areas of Haryana than elsewhere. There has been a tradition of fierce patriarchy in this region as in some parts of north India (Dreze and Sen, 1996). In patriarchal cultures, son preference intensifies in the transition period when fertility is declining (Dasgupta and Visaria, 1996).

These sex determination tests are most profound not only among the educated ones but among uneducated people also. There is an example in the UNFPA (United Nations Population Fund) supported study on 'Infanticide in Rajasthan – Causes and Practices' – a woman undertook nine sex determination tests and had eight pregnancies terminated. She died two days after giving birth to a son. She was a teacher in a public school and married to a senior executive in a multinational company. Birth of a male child is also preferred in developed capitalist and socialist societies. In India, culture is the main reason for the desire to have a son to obtain passport to heaven but in other countries like in China, Chinese couples accept a one-child family but the child has to be male. Dr Ronald Edrison, who has clinics for pre-selection tests in many developed and developing countries, said that out of 263 couples who approached him, 248 selected boys and 15 selected girls (Patel, 1988). In Germany, sons are known as 'Stemer Halter', i.e. those who continue the family. Even in USA, Russia, and UK, parents still prefer boys so that the name of family continues.

Neglect of girl child is probably thought out by men or fathers but studies show that in some caste groups and regions, mothers also do not want to give birth to daughters or girl child. Tulsi Patel's (2004) study on sex determination shows unfavourable solemn and outright rejection of mothers giving birth to daughters, barring the first daughter in some cases. This tendency is increasing among the prospering middle and lower castes in several districts in Uttar Pradesh and Madhya Pradesh. These castes, including the other backward castes, in their attempts are emulating higher caste practices. L.S. Vishwanath's (1998) paper revealed colonial records acknowledging the active role of communities in female infanticide. Another study in

Maharashtra shows that here women actively participate in the process of aborting female foetuses (Patel, 1988).

Causes of Female Foeticide

Female foeticide is a symptom of increasing crime against women. It would be manifestly wrong if we conclude that female foeticide is a matter of medical technology alone. There is no doubt that easy access to ultrasonography has been largely responsible for the spread of female foeticide throughout the country. Studies indicate that there is preference for sons in South Korea, Pakistan, India, Turkey, Mexico, Taiwan and China. In India, often the alibi is offered that families prefer boys to girls just because according to them boys provide security to the aged parents. Some people think a girl means accumulation of sufficient resources for the dowry; the parents have to give away, when the girl gets married. Therefore, the parents think that the girl is a financial burden for them, whereas the boy is an asset who fetches a fabulous dowry for the parents. From the cultural point of view is the concept of 'Vanshodharak', a male child to perform last rites in Hindus and carry forward. Certain communities want to get rid of female child compelled by the circumstances of dehumanizing poverty, unemployment, superstition and illiteracy. As Mira Shiva (2002) maintains, many women opted for female foeticide not because they were heartless but because they were genuinely concerned about the fate of girls who were increasingly subjected to eve-teasing, molestation and sexual harassment and, after marriage, exposed to the risk of bride burning and dowry death, in the unending demand for dowry from our emerging consumerist society. This calls for a good look at gender issues in all their ramifications in our increasingly dysfunctional society.

Consequences of Female Foeticide

Pre-natal sex determination with the intention of preventing female births must be viewed as a manifestation of violence against women, a violation of their human rights. The pregnant woman, though often equally anxious to have a boy, is frequently pressured to undergo such procedures. Many women suffer from psychological trauma as a result of forcibly undergoing repeated abortions. More generally, demographers warn that in the next twenty years, there will be a shortage of brides in the marriage market mainly because of the adverse juvenile sex ratio, combined with an overall decline in fertility. While fertility is declining more rapidly in urban and educated families, nevertheless the preference for male children remains strong. For these families, modern medical technologies are within easy reach. Thus, selective abortion and sex selection are becoming more common.

In rural areas, as the number of marriageable women declines, men would tend to marry younger women, leading to a rise in fertility rates and thus a high rate of population growth. The abduction of girls is an associated phenomenon. *Hindustan Times* recently reported that young girls from Assam and West Bengal are kidnapped and sold into marriage in neighbouring Haryana.

The impact on society should not be underestimated. According to Chinese estimates, by 2020, there are likely to be 40 million unmarried young men, called guang guan or 'bare branches', in China because of the adverse sex ratio. A society with a preponderance of unmarried young men is prone to particular dangers. More women are likely to be exploited as sex workers. Increase in molestations and rape cases is an obvious result. The sharp rise in sex crimes in Delhi has been attributed to the unequal sex ratio.

Legislative Actions

Until 1970, the provisions contained in the Indian Penal Code (IPC) governed the law on abortion. The Indian Penal Code, 1860 permitted 'legal abortions' without criminal intent and in good faith for the express purpose of saving the life of the mother. Liberalization of abortion laws was also advocated as one of the measures of population control. With these considerations, the Medical Termination of Pregnancy Act was passed in July 1971, which came into force in April 1972. This law was conceived as a tool to let the pregnant women decide on the number and frequency of children. It further gave them the right to decide on having or not having the child. However, this good intentioned step was being used to force women to abort the female child. To arrest this evil, the Forum Against Sex Determination and Sex Pre-selection (FASDSP), a broad forum of feminist and human rights groups, was formed in 1984, and it has been lobbying for legislation to ban the practice. In 1988, the state of Maharashtra passed an Act banning pre-natal diagnostic practices. On 20 September 1994, Parliament enacted the Pre-Natal Diagnostic Techniques (Regulation and Prevention of Misuse) Act, which came into force from January 1996 and has been amended twice since then, first in 1996 and again in 2003 and was renamed the Pre-Conception and Pre-Natal Diagnostic Techniques (Prohibition of Sex Selection) Act, 1994 (PCPNDT Act). Despite this legislation, the Child Sex Ratio has become even more masculine. It also provided for mandatory registration of genetic counselling centres, clinics, hospitals, nursing homes, etc. Thus, both these laws were meant to protect the childbearing function of the woman and legitimize the purpose for which pre-natal tests and abortions could be carried out. However, in practice we find that these provisions have been misused and are proving against the interest of the females.

Government and many organizations campaigned against this brutal practice. On 11 December 2001, the Supreme Court had directed 5 multinational companies – Philips, Symonds, Toshiba, Larsen and Toubro and Wipro CE – to give names and addresses of the clinics and persons in India to whom they have sold the machines in past five years. And it was a strict order to authorities to regularly check these clinics and their activities to prevent female foeticide. It was reported that after that, not a single ultrasound machine had been impounded in Delhi (*Statesman*, 3 February 2002). On 29

January 2002, health secretaries of Punjab, Haryana, Delhi, Bihar, Uttar Pradesh, Maharashtra, Gujarat, Andhra Pradesh, Kerala, Rajasthan and West Bengal were lined up before the Supreme Court and asked to initiate steps to curb female foeticide. After that state governments were directed to take immediate action if such machines are being used in the clinics without licences and the machines are to be seized and sealed for the time being (Bose, 2001). But after so many measures, this system of aborting the female foetus could not be stopped. Many private clinics are flourishing through their business of sex determination test.

Despite the implementation of the amended Pre-Conception and Pre-Natal Diagnostic Techniques Act (2003), there has been a steady decline in India's female sex ratio. A study was conducted in Maharashtra (30 September 2004) which shows that the districts with more than 100 sonography centres, showed a higher decline in child sex ratio (CSR) in comparison to other districts. The average sex ratio with more than 100 sonography centres is 901 and for districts with less than 100 sonography centres is 937.

Measures to Reduce Female Foeticide

Confronted with this situation, it is high time to take preventive measures against female foeticide. Both local leadership and government agencies should plan a concerted long-term programme aimed at the educational and socio-economic advancement of the community, e.g. by social welfare and poverty alleviation programmes, to improve the economic status of women. To wean the people away from the traditional practices, voluntary organizations should come forward to promote social education and awareness among the people through cultural programmes and public debate, etc.

The practice of dowry at the time of marriage should also be eliminated through education and concept of equality of sexes. Adult education has to be promoted. Laws relating to coil ferment of equal rights with regard to parental property should be implemented in the right spirit so that the stigma of liability attached to girlhood and womanhood could be eradicated forever. It is a challenge today to initiate a vibrant, effective campaign against female foeticide. Organizations and individuals with different priorities and ideological beliefs have to rally together to battle powerful patriarchal forces operating within the institutions of the family and civil society.

However, the national law against pre-natal diagnostic technique is a positive step which enabled the National Human Rights Commission to direct the Medical Council of India to take action against doctors found abusing pre-natal diagnostic techniques. There is a need for sustained campaigning and active monitoring of the act. State governments should realize the importance and priority of the law. Structures for implementation of the 1994 law need to be created at the district level. Volunteers have to be actively mobilized to monitor registration and functioning of sex determination clinics at different districts. Cases have to be filed against the violators and social consciousness has to be raised against the crime. Members of the society and the religious leaders have a positive role in creating a morally reformed society. The long-term task is to foster a culture of goodness and human dignity which inoculates individuals and institutions against the infection of this despicable human practice.

Conclusion

Female foeticide is aborting the female baby in the mother's womb. Foeticide is the legacy and contribution of the progress made by medical science. With the advent of privatization and commercialization, the use of pre-natal diagnostic technologies is growing into a thriving business in India. It is a grave problem that affects the life and health of society. The misuse of technology simply reinforces the secondary status given to girl children in such a way that they are culled out even before they are born. It is, therefore, essential that these socio-cultural factors be tackled by changing the thought process through awareness generation, mass appeal and social action. In addition to this, all concerned, i.e. the religious and social leaders, voluntary organizations, women's groups, socially responsible media, the doctors, the Medical Council/Association (by enforcing medical ethics and penalties on deviant doctors) and the law enforcement personnel should work in a coordinated way.

References

Arnold, Fred, M.K. Choe and T.K. Roy. 1998. 'Son-Preference, the Family Building Process and Child Mortality in India', *Population Studies*, Vol. 52, pp. 301–15.

Bose, A. 2001. *India's Billion Plus People: 2001 Census Highlights, Methodology and Media Coverage*, New Delhi: B.R. Publishing Corporation.

——. 2006. 'Female Foeticide: A Civilizational Collapse', in Tulsi Patel (ed.), *Sex Selective Abortion in India: Gender, Society and New Reproductive Technologies*, New Delhi: Sage Publications.

Dagar, Rainuka. 2006. 'Rethinking Female Foeticide: Perspective and Issues', in Tulsi Patel (ed.), *Sex Selective Abortion in India: Gender, Society and New Reproductive Technologies*, New Delhi: Sage Publications.

Dasgupta, M. and P.N.M. Bhat. 1997. 'Fertility Decline and Increased Manifestation of Sex Bias in India', *Population Studies*, Vol. 51, pp. 307–15.

Diaz, A.A. 1988. 'Amniocentesis and Female Foeticide', *Bulletin of the Indian Federation of Medical Guild*, 5 July.

Dreze, Jean and Amartya Sen. 1996. 'India: Economic Development and Social Opportunity', *Journal of Political Economy*, Vol. 107, pp. 1275–1304.

Dutta, Subhabrate. 2001. 'Child Sex Ratio: The Grim Picture', *Social Welfare*, November, pp. 17–24.

Gangrade, K.D. 1988. 'Sex Determination: A Critique', *Journal of Social Change*, Vol. 18, No. 3, pp. 63–70.

George, Sabu. 2000. 'Female Foeticide in India', *Health Action*, Vol. 13, No. 9, pp. 23–26.

Mies, Maria. 1980. *Indian Women and Patriarchy*, New Delhi: Concept Publishing Company.

Miller, Barbara D. 1997. *The Endangered Sex: Neglect of Female Children in Rural North India*, New Delhi: Oxford University Press.

Nair, G. Ravindran. 1991. 'Eternal Injustice Against Half the World', *Social Welfare*, February–March, pp. 32–37.

Patel, Tulsi. 2004. 'Missing Girls in India', *Economic and Political Weekly*, February, pp. 887–89.

——. 2007. *Sex Selective Abortion in India: Gender, Society and New Reproductive Technologies*, New Delhi: Sage Publications.

Patel, Vibhuti. 1988. 'Sex Determination and Sex Pre-selection Tests: Abuse of Advanced Technology', in Rehana Ghadially (ed.), *Women in Indian Society*, New Delhi: Sage Publications.

Perwez, Shahid, Jeffery Roger and Jeffery Patricia. 2012. 'Declining Sex Ratio and Sex Selection in India: A Demographic Epiphany?', *Economic and Political Weekly*, Vol. XLVII, No. 33, 18 August.

Sangari, Kumkum. 2012. 'Settled Alibis and Emerging Contradictions: Sex Selection, Dowry and Domestic Violence', *Economic and Political Weekly*, Vol. XLVII, No. 34, pp. 39–41.

Shiva, Mira. 2002. *Skirting the Issues: The Girl Child Seen but Not Heard*, New Delhi: VHAI.

Sudha, S. and S. Irudaya Rajan. 1999. 'Female Demographic Disadvantage in India 1981–1991: Sex Selective Abortions and Female Infanticide', *Development and Change*, Vol. 30, No. 6, pp. 585–618.

Visaria, Leela. 2006. 'Deficit of Girls in India: Can It Be Attributed to Female Selective Abortion?', in Tulsi Patel (ed.), *Sex Selective Abortion in India: Gender, Society and New Reproductive Technologies*, New Delhi: Sage Publications.

Vishwanath, L.S. 1998. 'Efforts of Colonial State to Suppress Female Infanticide: Use of Sacred Texts Generation of Knowledge', *Economic and Political Weekly*, 9 May, pp. 1004–12.

Zheng, Yi et al. 1993. 'Causes and Implication of the Increase in China's Reported Sex Ratio and Birth', *Population and Development Review*, Vol. 19, No. 2, pp. 283–302.

11

Girl Child Discrimination Since Conception of Life

Role of Laws and Government Policies

Sonu Dehmiwal

The attitude of the community towards the woman has social significance in any society. The position of women community has been a fluctuating subject since the early ages. With the ups and downs in the Hindu society, the status of women has been affected (Jayapalan, 2001). Majority of the societies are patriarchal in nature except very few matriarchal societies. It means that the male of the species of homo sapiens considers himself superior to the female in spite of the unique ability of the female to prorogate and nurture the species with little cooperation from the male. In a patriarchal, male-dominated society like ours, the preference for a male child is inherent in the Indian psyche as he perpetuates the family man and line. Besides the mistaken notion that he brings salvation to the parents in the hereafter by carrying out proper rituals at their death, he is considered as a bread-winner and support in the old age. A girl, on the other hand, usually leaves the family at marriage for her husband's home. In a sense, she is considered merely a transitory member of a family and only indirectly participates in building its strengths and prestige. Women are taught to believe that birth of a son is desirable not only as the first child but preferably all her children. Society gives open sanction to these attitudes and another girl grows up accepting her subordinate status in the family. No wonder in such a situation mothers too are pressured to committing female infanticide and foeticide.

Female Foeticide and Infanticide

One of the most common and simple mechanisms of eliminating the girl child is 'female foeticide'. It is the act of determining the sex of the child in the womb and if it is found to be a female, to get the same aborted. 'Foeticide' means the destruction of the foetus at any time prior to birth. Infanticide means the unlawful destruction of a newly-born child and is regarded as murder in the eyes of law (Parikh, 2002). Foetus means an human embryo, after the third month of pregnancy until birth. Female foeticide, also known as sex-selective abortion by the use of medical technology, identifies the sex of the foetus and selectively aborts female foetuses. Scientific technology facilitates a series of pre-natal diagnostic tools to identity and cure any potential birth defects but has also been misused especially in our country for sex-selective abortion.

The practice of killing children at birth is known as infanticide. It is mostly done in case of birth of a baby girl. Some of the methods used to eliminate girl babies after their birth care are: poisoning, throat splitting, starvation, and drawing, etc. At the same time, many girl children are left abandoned in the garbage dump, sewer or anywhere to be mauled by dogs. There is wide coverage in print and electronic media about the heinous crime that takes place all over.

There is a prohibitory norm that *'no human being can take the life of another human being'*. Now the question arises – whether the killing of a foetus amounts to taking the 'life' of another 'human being'?

Morally speaking, killing of a foetus is not the same as killing an infant; we do not get as normally outraged by an abortion of a foetus as we do when a child has been killed. Legally as well, the killing of an infant is homicide, whereas killing a foetus is not homicide but ought to be a special offence against human life. The offence of foeticide must therefore be punished unless there is an excuse or justification for the same. Moreover, as Lord Mahavira has said, the age of a child starts in the womb of mother from the day of conception. To count the age of child from the day of birth is just for our convenience; it starts right at the time of conception (*Aayu ka Praramb Garbh me hi ho jata hai. Janam ke baad Aayu ka Ginnah Lokik korm hai*) (Saurbsagar, 2008).

Reasons for Discrimination Against Girl Child

The root causes for discrimination against females in the form of foeticide and infanticide are complex and reflect diverse political, economical, social, cultural and religious practices. They include:

Preference for male child: In India, particularly in the north–western regions, there is a strong preference for sons for various reasons, including religious and economic ones. The sons are considered economically advantageous for a family. They have a much higher rate of employment than girls, thereby benefitting their families through their wages. Apart from the economic assistance to the family, the sons bring dowry at the time of their marriage through their wife and often continue to live in the home with their parents and help them in sickness and infirmity (Kumari et al., 1990).

- *Pressure from husband and relatives:* In Indian society, usually the father holds primary responsibility in the family for all practical purposes. The hard reality of life within the society is that relations in a family are to be tackled by the male members. So, it is quite natural that the male member, especially the husband, would make up a mindset against the birth of a female child and they will prevail upon the females and force the mother to go in for abortion.

- *Evil of dowry:* Some people think that to have a girl means accumulation of sufficient resources for dowry; the parents have to spend a lot on a girl's marriage. Therefore, she is taken as a financial burden, whereas the boy is an asset who fetches a fabulous dowry for them.
- *Illiteracy among the women:* In India, a woman is not conscious about her own identity. She is unable to recognize her role in resolving her problems because of the prevalence of orthodoxy system. The mindset of girls and women is shaped by cultural and institutional notions whereby they consider themselves as inferior citizens, and girl child as a second class commodity. On the basis of this reason, women themselves decide against bringing girls into this cruel world.
- *Higher education:* The higher education in the society reveals that the people who are more educated are always inclined to the more sex-selective abortion.
- *Richness of people:* The higher income group is more diverted to the new reproductive technology, i.e. ultrasound to detect the female foetus because rich people have no bar of any financial matter. They want the son only for the heir of their property, but in case of female, all their property may be transferred to their grooms. This also leads them to detect the foetus of the female and abort them.

Consequences of Female Foeticide

Female foeticide cannot be viewed in isolation. It has to be viewed in the greater context of gender discrimination and atrocities against women (Sunita and Elamon, 2000). In such circumstances, 'is it not desirable that a woman dies rather than be ill-treated? Is it really better to be born and be left to die than be killed as a foetus? Does the birth of lakhs or even millions of unwanted girls improve the status of women? As a crime against society, female foeticide has a number of adverse effects upon the society. It can be broadly summarized as follows:

- As a device of selective reproduction, it will seriously upset the demographic balance in the society and after a point of time, the number of females in the society will be very few compared to that of males.
- It will result in the decline of values in life and overall social degradation, which in turn will promote social evil and offences against women like rape, exploitation, kidnapping, etc.
- The reduced sex ratio will result in a fewer number of marriageable women and the institution of '*polyandry*' will resurface and that would lead to tension in families and later on in the society.
- Low female sex ratio will generate sexual starvation among the males and it will help to flourish the business of prostitution and immoral trafficking. The increase in prostitution will lead to spread of venereal diseases and would pose serious problems like spread of AIDS, etc.
- Women will not be permitted to go out of their houses on account of increased crimes against them and consequently they will be deprived of better education, employment opportunities and economic freedom.
- Continued practice of female foeticide will give rise to emergence of black market in service and medical profession.

The whole issue of selective elimination of females has to be understood in the wider perspective of gender issues and in the context of increasing violence against women and girls and child protection. Undeniably, sex selection is an extreme form of discrimination and violence against girls. The adverse child sex ratio reflects the real status of the girl child in the country, challenging the constitutional and policy commitments of equality and non-discrimination. It is a gross violation of the human rights of the girl child.

Further, to believe that it is better to kill a female foetus than to give birth to an unwanted female child is not only short-sighted but also fatalistic. By this logic, it is better to kill poor people or Third World Masses rather than let them suffer in poverty and deprivation. This logic also presumes that social evils like dowry are God-given and we cannot do anything about them. Hence, victimize the victim.

Sex Ratio at Birth

The sex ratio at birth is determined by the sex ratio at the time of conception and intra-uterine mortality, which may be spontaneous as well as induced. At the time of conception, the masculine sex ratio is very high. However, the spontaneous intra-uterine mortality of the male foetus is very high. On the other hand, in recent years, induced intra-uterine mortality of female foetus appears to have increased because of sex-selective abortions gaining alarming proportions in some parts of the country. It has been estimated that in the absence of induced intra-uterine mortality, males outnumber females at birth. The global norm is 105 male births for every 100 female births (Census of India) but this gap is widening over time. The low sex ratio at birth in India is the reflection of the practice of sex-selective abortions (Chaurasia and Gulati, 2007).

According to the Government of India's first periodic report to the UN Committee on the Rights of the Child, 2001, every year, 12 million girls are born – three million of whom do not survive to see their 15th birthday. About one-third of these deaths occur in the first year of life. UN figures out that about 7,50,000 girls are aborted every year in India. Abortion rates are increasing in almost 80 per cent of the Indian states, mainly Punjab and Haryana. According to a recent report by the United Nations Children's Fund (UNICEF), up to 50 million females are missing from population of India as a result of systematic gender discrimination. In most countries in the world, there are approximately 105 female births for every 100 males. But in India, in almost all the states, the population of females is less than the males in all age groups.

International Framework to Protect Girl Child

1. *The United Nations Convention on the Rights of Child:* Article 6 of the Convention on the Rights of Child provides that the State shall recognize that every child has the inherent right to life. It also casts a duty upon the State to ensure the possible survival and development of the child. Further, the Convention casts a duty upon the State to ensure that no child should be discriminated on the basis of sex. Now the question arises – whether under the said convention, the definition of child being a 'human being up to the age of 18 years' was intended to include an unborn child? The answer to this question must be yes, as 'up to 18 years' would include the period both before and after the birth. Also, it can be seen in Article 24 which urges the State to ensure proper pre-natal care for mothers that the Convention on Rights of Child is concerned with the interest of child even before it is born.
2. *The Convention on the Elimination of All Forms of Discrimination Against Women (CEDAW):* Adopted in 1979, it is the most extensive and widely-ratified international agreement promoting the rights of girls and women. The CEDAW is considered to be equivalent to an international Bill of rights for women, defining what constitutes discrimination and providing an agenda for action. It states the negative consequences of female discrimination and seeks full equality between men and women in all fields of political, economic, social and cultural life. States that have ratified CEDAW must take concrete steps such as enacting laws, establishing women's rights commissions and creating conditions to ensure that human rights of girls and women are fulfilled. Their progress is monitored by the UN Committee on the Elimination of Discrimination Against Women.

National Framework

1. *The Indian Penal Code, 1860:* Abortion was first penalized under the IPC, which makes the causing of a

miscarriage (if it is not done in good faith to save the life of a woman) an offence punishable with imprisonment up to seven years. The code makes both the women who undergo the abortion (voluntarily) as well as the abortionist liable to punishment.

In case it is carried out without the consent of the woman, then punishment of 10 years is prescribed in the Act and if it is carried out with the consent of the women the person carrying out such an abortion is punishable for life and if death of a woman is caused by the Act, then the offence will be punishable with imprisonment up to 10 years.[2] The most important provision regarding foeticide is the recognition of the foetus as '*quick*'.[3] If a foetus is killed after it becomes 'quick', it is punishable with 10 years' imprisonment. Further, doing of any act with intent to prevent the child from being born alive is punishable with 10 years' imprisonment. Section 316 of IPC deals with the cases in which by doing any act, death of a woman is caused thereby causing the death of a '*quick*' unborn child will be punishable with 10 years' imprisonment.

Furthermore, exposing and abandoning the child below 12 years of age is punishable with seven years of imprisonment. And concealing the birth of a child by secretly disposing of her/his body is punishable with two years' imprisonment under Section 318 of IPC.

2. *Code of Medical Ethics:* It was constituted by the Indian Parliament in the Medical Council Act, 1956. The relevant section of the Code of Medical Ethics states: 'On no account, sex determination test shall be undertaken with the intent to terminate the life of a female foetus developing in her mother's womb, unless there are other absolute indicators for termination of pregnancy as specified in the Medical Termination of Pregnancy Act, 1971. Therefore, any act of termination of pregnancy of normal female foetus, amounting to female foeticide, shall be regarded as professional misconduct on the part

of the physician, leading to penal punishment besides rendering him liable to criminal proceedings as per the provisions of this Act (clause 7.6).'

3. *Medical Termination of Pregnancy Act, 1971 (MTPA):* Amniocentesis was first started in India in 1974 as a part of sample survey conducted at the All India Institute of Medical Sciences (AIIMS), New Delhi, to detect foetal abnormalities. These tests were later stopped by the Indian Council of Medical Research (ICMR), but their value had leaked out by then and 1979 saw the first sex determination clinic opening in Amritsar, Punjab. Even though women organizations across the country took up cudgels to put a stop to this new menace, they were helpless because of the MTPA. This is because the amniocentesis test was claimed to be used for detection of foetal abnormalities, which was permitted by the MTPA. According to the MTPA, if any abnormality is detected between 12 to 18 weeks of gestational period in the foetus, an abortion can be legally carried out up to 20 weeks of pregnancy (Zaidi, 2006).

   In the absence of any law, all that the government could do was to issue circulars prior to 1985, banning the misuse of medical technology for sex determination in all government institutions. This, however, led to the mushrooming of private clinics all over the country. In 1986, the Forum Against Sex Determination and Sex Pre-selection (FASDSP), a social action group in Mumbai, initiated a campaign. Succumbing to public pressure, the Maharashtra government enacted the Maharashtra Regulation of Pre-Natal Diagnostic Techniques Act 1988, the first anti-sex determination drive in the country. This was followed by a similar Act being introduced in Punjab in May 1994.

   Both these were however repealed by the enactment of a central legislation, the Pre-Natal Diagnostic Techniques (Regulation and Prevention of Misuse) Act, 1994.

4. *Pre-Natal Diagnostic Techniques (Regulation and Prevention of Misuse) Act, 1994 (PNDT):* In 1994, the Centre passed this Act but it was only in 1996 that it came into operation. Under the Act, pre-natal diagnostic scans are permitted solely to detect genetic abnormalities. The Act forbids sex determination tests. It also prohibits any advertisements relating pre-natal determination of sex and prescribes punishment for its contravention. The person who contravenes the provisions of this Act is punishable with imprisonment up to 5 years and fine up to 50,000.

   In 2001, a PIL was filed in the Supreme Court. The court directed the state governments to enforce the PNDT Act and file an affidavit indicating the status of action taken under the Act. Certain guidelines were also issued to the Central Government like:

   - The Central Government is directed to create public awareness against the practice of pre-natal determination of sex, etc.
   - The Central Government is also directed to implement with all vigour and zeal the PNDT Act and the rules framed in 1996.

   Further, direction was also issued to the Central Supervisory Board (CSB), state governments and the appropriate authorities.

   It was only in 2002, i.e. eight years after the PNDT Act was passed, that the Medical Council of India (MCI) authorized under Section 23(2) of the Act to take action against any erring medical practitioner ... performing sex-determination tests 'with the intent to terminate the life of a female foetus' as professional misconduct. On 17 January 2003, India amended its Pre-Natal Diagnostic Techniques (Regulation and Prevention of Misuse) Act, 1994 that was renamed as Pre-Conception and Pre-Natal Diagnostic Techniques Act (PCPNDT) of 2002.

5. *Pre-Conception and Pre-Natal Diagnostic Techniques Act (PCPNDT) of 2002:* The reason of few convictions under

the old Act of PNDT, 1994 and the grave misuse of scientific technology by the rich like 'sperm-washing' compelled amendment in the Act. This new Act is designed to strengthen the provisions of the previous Act.

Bringing into the ambit of the Act emerging techniques for pre-conception and sex-selection, such as sperm separation and pre-implantation genetic diagnosis, increasing the fine and additional provisions for the suspension and cancellation of the registration of violators, the law targets the medical profession, the so-called 'supply' side of the practice of sex-selection. Manufacturers of ultrasound equipment are now required to sell their products only to registered clinics, and all ultrasonographers now have to maintain records of all tests conducted by them.

Government Incentives

The declining sex ratio has been a matter of concern for policy-makers, social scientists, women's groups, and social activists. A sequel to the non-starter *'Balika Samriddhi Yojana'* of 1997 in which cash payments to poor families were taking long to be disbursed, the new scheme offers money to parents who fulfill four conditions linked to a girl's survival and welfare. These are – ensuring her birth and registering it, completing her immunization, educating her and delaying her marriage till 18 years. The scheme was launched as a pilot in 10 economically backward blocks of Andhra Pradesh, Chhattisgarh, Jharkhand, Bihar and Odisha. The Eleventh Five Year Plan has already provided ₹ 9.11 crore to benefit 99,000 girls under the Scheme. As far as northern region is concerned, the government of Haryana had announced a price of ₹ 5 lakh to the panchayat which makes the strenuous efforts to balance the sex ratio. Further, a *'Jacha Bacha Scheme'* has also been launched to promote safe institutional delivery, increase female sex ratio and ensure gender equality and women's empowerment. Under the scheme, female multipurpose health workers, staff nurses and medical officers attending to childbirths will be given performance-based incentives.

We know that 24 January is observed as the National Girl Child Day and there are government incentives to protect the girl child. According to UNICEF report 2009, 'What we need is action on ground. Key flagship schemes of the UPA government like the Integrated Child Protection Scheme (ICPS) are not taking off. In such a situation, what is the meaning of having one more day dedicated to girls? It is a shame' (Tandon, 2009). Alarmed by the increasing female foeticide cases, both the Centre and the state governments have formulated new policies to curb this menace. A slew of measures, including monitoring of the use of ultrasound machines and setting up state inspection committees to check pre-natal sex determination, have been undertaken by the government.

Faced with the daunting task of improving the sex ratio and curbing female foeticide, the Rajasthan government is planning to draft a new policy as the steps taken so far in this direction have not borne the desirable results. Chief Minister Ashok Gehlot on 11 May 2012 announced the formulation of a 'girl child policy' in the state, aimed at making the government's stand clear on issues like female foeticide, sex determination and the implementation of related laws. For the expeditious disposal of female foeticide cases, he announced setting up of fast-track courts. And all this happened with the help of Aamir Khan's show '*Satyameva Jayate*' that aired on Star Plus channel.

Expressing concern over the practice of female foeticide, the Delhi Chief Minister, Sheila Dixit, on 11 July 2012 said her government was considering imposing 'heavy' fine and stricter punishment for those involved in such crimes. The continuing serious decline in the 0–6 sex ratio in India, indicates that the government's policies are ineffective. The two-child policy has got mixed up with female foeticide. Government slogans like '*Beti ya beta, dono ek hain*' make little sense. And financial sops for couples having a girl child can make no dent in the traditional preference for sons in India.

Issues Relating to Female Foeticide

The seeds sown by the society will come back to haunt the society and the sharp fall in child sex ratio is a symptom of the disease which any sane society should not ignore (Ram et al., 2011). Foremost, it is 18 years since the enactment of the Pre-Natal Diagnostic Techniques (Regulation and Prevention of Misuse) Act, 1994. It is also over 10 years since the more comprehensive, amended Pre-Conception and Pre-Natal Diagnostic Techniques (PCPNDT) Act, 2002 came into existence. Yet, enforcing the law has proved to be a major challenge given the resistance from the unethical medical practitioners. Effective implementation of PCPNCT Act needs to be assured through ensuring registration, curbing the spread of mobile ultrasound and regulating sale of new machines.

The appropriate authorities are ineffective and are not held accountable by the government and civil society and the powerful doctors' lobby. Clinics that have been sealed for breaking the law have been re-opened within a few days. Lawbreakers have got away after paying a fine of just ₹ 1,000. Another problem is that the appropriate authorities do not know their functions and responsibilities. They do not have the necessary experience and expertise in legal matters. Deputing of medical professionals has not been an effective way to check the practice of sex determination. Survival of girl child is not part of the reproductive health agenda and finds no mention in the Reproductive Child Health (RCH) programme.

Effective and strong implementation of the law should go side by side with reviews of policy and development strategies. We should advocate public acceptance of the reality that the continuing discrimination against the girl child is not just due to 'deep-rooted socio-cultural practices' but is exacerbated by short-sighted and unsound public policies in population and their accompanying development packages. One possible way could be job reservation for women, because without economic empowerment, political empowerment will not be enough.

Lastly, the solution lies in raising the status of women, making the presence of women felt, and actively contributing to raising their status in decision-making at community and family level. Young boys and girls should be motivated to contribute to raising the status of women. Right from the very early ages, boys should be made to do all the things the girls are 'expected' to do so that these fixed role images can be eliminated. Society must appreciate and highlight the cases where the old parents are living with daughters, who are not only looking after them but also performing the last rites. This will lead to equality between men and women and once they enjoy equal status with men, then not only will the sex ratio improve, but the girl child will have her equal share in the family as well as society.

Notes

1. Only in Kerala and Puducherry the number of females is 1,058 and 1,001 per 1,000 males, respectively.
2. For the purpose, a woman under misconception, a woman of unsound mind, a woman in an intoxicated state, and a girl below 12 years of age cannot give consent.
3. Quickening is the name applied to the peculiar sensation experienced by a woman in about the fourth or fifth month of pregnancy. The symptoms are popularly ascribed to the first perception of the movement of the foetus.

References

Chaurasia, Alok Ranjan and S.C. Gulati. 2007. *India: The State of Population*, New Delhi: Oxford University Press, p. 82.

Council of Social Development. 2006. *India Social Development Report 2006*, Delhi: Oxford University Press, p. 155.

Iyer, S. 2001. *Killing the Unborn: Law and Morality*, Salem: Cauvery Publications, p. 130.

Jayapalan, N. 2001. *Women and Human Rights*, New Delhi: Atlantic Publishers.

Kumari, R., R. Singh and A. Dubey. 1990. *Grouping Up in Rural India: Problems and Needs of Adolescent Girls*, New York: Advent.

Parikh, C.K. 2002. *Parikh's Text Book of Medical Jurisprudence, Forensic Medicine and Toxicology*, Bombay: CBS Publishers, p. 72.

Ram, F., S. Unisa and T.V. Sekher. 2011. *Population, Gender and Reproductive Health*, Rawat Publications, Jaipur and Delhi, p. 118.

Saurbsagar, Digamber Jain Muni. 2008. *Mat Kuchlo Masoom Kali Ko*, Vol. VIII, p. 18. (Please check this reference again and complete it?)

Sharma, Mahesh. 2008. 'Anything for a Boy: Rich Prefer "Sperm-washing"', *The Tribune*, 7 March.

Sunita and J. Elamon. 2000. *Medical Technology: Its Uses and Abuses in Trivandrum City*, Thiruvananthapuram: Achutha Menon Centre for Health Science Studies, pp. 329–30.

Tandon, Aditi. 2008. 'Case of Missing Daughter', *The Tribune*, 26 January.

——. 2009. 'Will It Improve Girls' Lot?', *The Tribune*, 20 January.

Zaidi, Zoya. 2006. 'Female Foeticide in India', *Sikhspectrum.com Quarterly*, Issue No. 24, May.

Index